48.95

THE BUSINESS
KNOWLEDGE
INVESTMENT

THE BUSINESS KNOWLEDGE INVESTMENT

Building
Architected Information

J. Alfred French

YOURDON PRESS
Prentice Hall Building
Englewood Cliffs, New Jersey 07632

Library of Congress Cataloging-in-Publication Data

French, J. Alfred
  The business knowledge investment : building architected
information / J. Alfred French.
    p.   cm.
  Includes bibliographical references.
  ISBN 0-13-091000-7
  1. Management--Communication systems--Data processing.
2. Management information systems. 3. Computer architecture.
I. Title.
HD30.335.F74 1990
658.4'038'011--dc20   89-38969
                                                          CIP

Editorial/production supervision: George Calmenson
Cover design: Wanda Lubelska Design
Manufacturing buyer: Mary Ann Gloriande

 © 1990 by Prentice-Hall, Inc.
A Division of Simon & Schuster
Englewood Cliffs, New Jersey 07632

The publisher offers discounts on this book when ordered in bulk
quantities. For more information, write:

Special Sales/College Marketing
Prentice-Hall, Inc.
College Technical and Reference Division
Englewood Cliffs, NJ 07632

BKA is an exclusive registered trademark
of Business Knowledge Architecture, Inc.

BKA* is the abbreviation for the
software product "Business Knowledge Advisor."

Printed in the United States of America

10 9 8 7 6 5 4 3 2 1

ISBN 0-13-091000-7

PRENTICE-HALL INTERNATIONAL (UK) LIMITED, *London*
PRENTICE-HALL OF AUSTRALIA PTY. LIMITED, *Sydney*
PRENTICE-HALL CANADA INC., *Toronto*
PRENTICE-HALL HISPANOAMERICANA, S.A., *Mexico*
PRENTICE-HALL OF INDIA PRIVATE LIMITED, *New Delhi*
PRENTICE-HALL OF JAPAN, INC., *Tokyo*
SIMON & SCHUSTER ASIA PTE. LTD., *Singapore*
EDITORA PRENTICE-HALL DO BRASIL, LTDA., *Rio de Janeiro*

Contents

To James Martin

Preface

Business knowledge is increasingly recognized by many leading corporations as a major asset of an enterprise.

When American companies first began to utilize computer systems, smart management initially concentrated on the advantages of replacing human functions with computer functions. The economies are obvious. Computers can calculate, file, sort, summarize, and retrieve faster than armies of clericals. Computers work three shifts, without fatigue, vacations, fringe benefits, unions, or pension funds.

However, such *functional productivity* was only the beginning of what is to come. *Knowledge productivity* has recently become a major focus of business managers. There is a growing recognition that business profits and productivity can be dramatically improved where business managers can be provided fast access to organized sets of related work, rules, and subject information of an enterprise.

Many computer software vendors have rushed to create computerized tools to assist businesses in creating better organized systems and information. CASE (computer-aided software engineering) is an acronym for computer tools that facilitate the organization of system components and the generation of computer programs.

Frequently, competing CASE tools and their consultants present a hodgepodge of metaphors without a suitable prelude to help the user to understand what they are and if or how they can be used to generate business profits. Initially, these tools seem to place more emphasis on graphics and technology than on business knowledge and results. Conversely, new knowledge tools should provide integrated *advice* and *prompting* directly to business operatives in order to facilitate more productive group activity.

Computers have been applied too frequently to only selected pieces of a business. Too many times, variances in incompatible hardware, software, communications, and functions inhibit the association of computerized business knowledge. Information developed for one business process (application) fails to fit or connect to another business process.

If gaps are discovered, complex and elaborate interfaces are created to bridge the oversights. Additional computer technicians are then required to maintain these bridges. Networks of business applications grow in complexity to the point where a single change requires changes to hundreds of parts in other systems. Most systems are static: They are not built to facilitate change, accommodate expansion, or identify what the change impacts.

Information inconsistencies go unexplained because so much logic is buried in long-forgotten computer programs. People are reluctant to touch these dinosaurs because of the fear that they might disrupt what is at least working. The originators are gone, the program language may be obsolete, and no documentation may exist to describe what is going on inside the machine. Frequently, old systems are left to run their course, even as new duplicate systems are implemented. The same scenario is repeated year after year, costing companies millions of dollars.

The processes of how information is related, how it is used, and what it really means are at best fuzzy. Without a global business perspective, the piecemeal approach can continue to increase company data handling budgets with little added return on investment (ROI). To function effectively, managers must have a practical understanding of this knowledge dilemma and what can be done to control it. All levels of management can provide leadership in computerization and direct its use toward improved profits and reduced costs.

As the passion and search for excellence continues, the need for knowledge preservation increases.

This book is for business managers. It is a step-by-step guide to business knowledge: its content, planning, relationships, meaning, and control. The author provides a clear and concise detailed handbook that takes you straight to the *why* you accumulate business knowledge as you invest in automation and then to the *how to* do it.

Whether you are planning new information investments or working with an existing information base, *knowledge* presents an integrated technique you can immediately use. You can preserve your own knowledge using architectural structures to

- Create your own information platforms
- Construct business rules
- Eliminate what costs time
- Acquire only what makes sense
- Provide a permanent knowledge investment

There are many examples that provoke creative thought and answer the following questions:

How can you identify and evaluate knowledge?
How is the entire company able to read the same message?
How can a data processing staff raise performance?
What does the context of a business model expose?
How does knowledge relate to profits?
What standards and disciplines are required?

You don't have to be a computer expert to create high-quality knowledge and information. You do need an understanding of a relational archetype like that presented in this idea book in order to communicate what must be done to establish the corporate peer networks of the future.

The author, J. Alfred French, maintains a heavy schedule of consulting and perfecting business knowledge inventories. For twenty years he has been a Director of Information Systems Development for several U.S. corporations. He is a past president of the Data Processing Management Association and the author of *Up the EDP Pyramid*. His paradigm, described in this book, has been utilized in actual business practice to affect knowledge productivity. Mr. French holds a BS in Industrial Management from the University of Illinois, an MBA from Northwestern University, and a CDP from the Institute of Certification of Computer Professionals.

Introduction

During many years of directing knowledge and information development for major U.S. corporations, I have witnessed million-dollar outlays to provide business data and to replace human functions with computer functions.

Some of these computer system projects resulted in excellent returns to companies in both reducing operating costs and increasing decision-making capabilities. Frequently, however, many of these efforts fell short of providing a permanent knowledge base to accelerate the competitive edge or provide added value for business productivity, performance, and resource utilization.

In my association with many chief executives, we have frequently discussed why some of our efforts were successful and why some systems resulted in million-dollar fiascos. We now have a clear picture of why. Primarily, it has been the best of intentions and technologies but the worst of strategies and techniques.

With the introduction of computer technology to business activities in the early 1960s, few pioneers could have foreseen the many cycles that would occur in automating and reautomating the same business applications again and again. This reiterative practice continues in many companies. The general ledger is an example of an application that has been replaced by package after package. These packages frequently duplicate much of what already exists. One-time savings may be achieved; however, most general ledger packages do not demonstrate how managers can actually

1. Increase sales, profits, product quality, and service
2. Reduce payroll or general expenses

Many production system replacements are technology driven by computer vendors who have created more computer power with lower-cost hardware. Frequently, new software packages are produced that can provide better (or at least more) information than existing programs. Tragically, managers are frequently not using what currently exists before they initiate more changes.

Both computer hardware and software require a considerable conversion investment before their proposed savings can be achieved. Related payroll costs can go unnoticed in the surge to adopt new hardware. Most new technology persists in automating more human functions rather than improving the knowledge of managers. Integrated knowledge to support human performance is sorely needed.

Business functions are facilitated by placing them on line with computer files. Systems that only accelerate transaction processing are frequently created. Examples of these processes are found in the reservation networks of airline, transport, lodging, banking, and leasing industries. The separation and stand-alone characteristics of transaction-oriented systems complicate the analysis of whether the transaction itself is profitable.

Duplication, redundancy, and reimplementation of separate application-oriented systems continue to fragment thinking and information. Global information opportunities go unnoticed in the surge to maintain, fix, or enhance a part here or a piece there.

Managers consistently proclaim that "we must get our people to work together more effectively." Yet, the group–peer productivity conflict is perpetuated by not ensuring that all departments are oriented to the same information infrastructure. Conflicting signals on different information scoreboards set managers at odds with each other. The synergistic profit potential is constrained.

Proof of information divergence is seen increasingly as each new round of technology recreates what already exists rather than building a standard foundation for expansion. Little attention is given to a shifting of mental gears: Only new, faster engines are perceived.

Because the mystique of computers has faded and their cost has fallen, operational managers are demanding personal computers but have nonintegrated ideas of how the machines can contribute to the total company profit. Hopefully they will eliminate their own jobs. More than likely they will create a couple of new jobs.

The replication, redundancy, and duplication goes on hardly noticed. A new perspective is required.

Thousands of Toms, Joes, and Debbies are spending hours of computer time developing tidbits of data, most of which will never be used to produce one cent of profit. Lower-cost computers arrive, but higher-cost, undirected talent offsets the potential productivity.

Almost everyone in business is scanning or toting thousands of lines of video screens or spreadsheets that should never have been produced. Why? "For the information, of course." "We need it to run the business." "We are saving hours of calculation time!" Never mind that we don't need to count the number of angles on the bulkhead at all. Simplification is needed, not volume or complexity.

The age of departmental analysts has arrived. Their mission is to increase productivity and reduce costs in their department. However, with each analyst preoccupied with only his or her square of the chessboard, the whole activity usually terminates in lunchroom debates, splitting hairs to the point of insensibility. These hidden staff costs are escalating as a percentage of total payroll.

But why do managers sleep? Are profits so good? Clearly there is fatigue, swamps/alligators, forests/trees, corporate cultures, and politics. Who wants to say they haven't thrown some microcomputers at the problem? It might seem backward to avoid the trend of information fragmentation.

Major opportunities are frequently lost because a global business metaphor does not exist to promote group-peer or company-to-company interaction.

A purpose of this book is to present a perspective needed to structure, plan, acquire, control, and preserve business knowledge at a dramatically lower cost. Business knowledge architecture is presented as a global and holistic platform to allow managers to work together more effectively, using standard architected information. Information overload and fragmentation are certain death in the long run.

In order to maximize computerized knowledge, a sampling of the objectives covered in this book includes

- Identifying and evaluating knowledge
- Unifying messages and information
- Giving improved performance recommendations for a data processing staff
- Establishing a business model and discussing ramifications
- Examining the relationship between knowledge and profits
- Incorporating requisite standards and disciplines

Part One is for business managers. It examines what information is, why it is a uniform force for profits, and how information presentation affects human performance and costs. The emphasis is placed on the shifting of responsibility for systems development from the data processing technician to the business manager.

Part Two is an original metaphor that exemplifies the levels of detail and standards required to build globally architected information and to computerize business knowledge. It is important to unite business managers and computer professionals with a relational *technique* so that they can globally organize, examine, and control their business knowledge and information *prior to* selecting diverse software, networks, computer hardware, or case tool implementation schemes.

Part Three describes the scope, phases, and activities of a global systems development cycle for business managers to utilize in their long-term business knowledge program implementation. Associated migration problems and considerations are described.

Each part of this book builds on a uniform terminology. Standard terminology is reinforced consistently throughout all the chapters and is needed to relate global knowledge domains to their lowest level of detail. The author urges business managers to read each chapter carefully (please do not skim over chapters) in order to avoid the loss of overall context and continuity.

Since most business managers will continue to invest heavily in information processing, knowledge about knowledge itself is a primary and critical prerequisite.

> A global economy demands a major business investment in knowledge workers, knowledge techniques, and knowledge tools.

THE BUSINESS
KNOWLEDGE
INVESTMENT

PART ONE

BUSINESS KNOWLEDGE AND PROFITS

The purpose of Part One is to describe the need to integrate management strategies, the activities of people, the functions of technology, and the preservation of knowledge.

Knowledge is a major asset of any business organization, yet many businesses do not treat it as such. Tangible assets of organizations such as buildings, equipment, investments, and cash are tightly controlled because their dollar value can be more precisely established. Knowledge is an intangible asset and is therefore more difficult to quantify, accumulate, or measure. Information per se only supports knowledge.

Business knowledge must relate to the way a business can be made more profitable. The story of knowledge management usually stops here. There is a general agreement about the subject but without the insight of what to do about it. A premise of this book is that business knowledge can be precisely defined, accumulated, preserved, measured, and controlled to dramatically enhance profits.

Recently, a few companies in the United States have begun to realize that knowledge management and its distribution are keys to profits and a long-term competitive advantage.

Knowledge management is a prerequisite, and a powerful force for, increased productivity. Some managements have heard pieces of the knowledge resource argument but believe it is a tired subject with no understandable solution. Actually, it is one of the most exciting challenges of the century.

Some managers have taken the time to understand the impact of knowledge *mis*management on their staff and on the bottom-line profits. How they came to this realization and why they are funding major long-term programs to structure their knowledge base is a subject of this book.

The knowledge connection to increased profits comes slowly. In a global economy, businesses achieve profits through increased productivity. Knowledge and information are complements by which people can achieve productivity by using technology in place of centralized multilayered management.

Unstructured information does not allow people to increase their aggregate productivity. In fact, without a highly organized base of information (uniformly interpretable by all) computer technology only produces *scrap data* that points people in conflicting directions. More "data" is simply counterproductive to the profit-making activity. More data is not synonymous with better information. Better information is not synonymous with knowledge. This distinction is not apparent from the outlays by many companies for a hodgepodge of undirected computer hardware, software, networks, and high-priced, ineffective staffs.

Many data processing organizations are bogged down in the technicalities of programming languages, data base file designs, changing computer hardware, control software, communications networks, applications packages, and associated activities.

Many managers have little insight into how knowledge and information enables business operatives to increase profits or to improve the intelligence of and insights to the business. Few have insights into how information must be organized in order to trigger improvements in knowledge and performance.

For knowledge and information to be organized, managers will have to lead a major companywide project. The case for business knowledge preservation will have to be made at the boardroom level. An in-depth discussion of the need for an information/knowledge construction technique will help serious management appreciate

1. The required investment
2. The steps to create it
3. The innovation to sustain it

MBWA (management by wandering around) may keep politicians busy in endless meetings with customers, vendors, and employees. However, the proactive business can only gain momentum by keeping acquired knowledge structured, updated, and in the hands of business managers.

A goal for business managers is to find ways to utilize technology using better techniques.

The 1940 ratio of four production employees to every one staff position has shifted to one production employee for five staff positions.

The current business challenge is to increase the productivity of the white-collar knowledge worker. To meet this challenge, managers must address information, work, attitudes, and team relationships.

The extension of and responsibility for information to the lowest levels of the organization is a key to productivity.

Chapter 1 (*why?*) focuses on knowledge and information about profits, information problems, and their associated costs.

Chapter 2 (*what?*) describes the scope of business knowledge, its classifications, and its integration needs.

Chapter 3 (*who?*) addresses the current and future roles of managers in knowledge construction and control.

Until business managers perceive (1) the effect that knowledge has on the total performance of the business and (2) the increasing costs of creating diverse islands of disjointed information, profit will be consumed by confusion resulting from the very technology by which it is produced.

> The lack of knowledge control has become a major liability of the business organization.
>
> Its transfer depends on standardization of context, semantics, and syntax.

Chapter 1

Business Knowledge: A Global Strategy

INTRODUCTION

Most managers can spell *knowledge*. Many managers believe they know something about it. Few believe they can do much about it, and most really never try. A knowledge structure is the first requirement to understanding the scope of knowledge. Each organization has its own unique characteristics. Because each company differs from others, its information needs also differ. This is probably why so many diverse computerized application packages require so much rework to adapt them to the needs of a company.

Many businesses have spent and will spend fortunes on piecemeal computer systems and packages that will never fit together and that will continue to be retrofitted to the point of complete breakdown before being discarded.

The basic underpinnings and foundations of business information and knowledge seem never to be traceable to the *profit* motive. The computer system creators are usually more oriented to a sequence of work to be transposed into computer functions. Islands of data files are assembled to support separate business applications but are not connected to the overall measurements of the total business. The perception of the whole is distorted by viewing only one piece at a time.

Many data experts are convincing managements that there is a package for each business application. They proclaim that every employee, customer, and vendor should be linked by microcomputers. The argument seldom exposes the primary need to structure a global information base prior to the automation of any one of the processes. Meanwhile, the technical community pursues new ways to create miles of spreadsheets and networks, regardless of the worth of the data or its impact on business personnel.

A basic premise of this chapter is that every manager and every employee of any business contribute marginally to business profits, and, in many cases, to a loss. The employee profit contribution relates directly to a function performed and the cost of performing it. What information is presented to an employee and how and when it is presented contribute to that degree of performance. The information provided determines

- What decisions will be made
- What priorities are established
- If actions are to be taken
- How quickly actions will occur

One of the most interesting phenomena of current business practice is the persistence of business operatives in asking for more, and a greater variety of, information. Current business functions are frequently isolated from each other and require only a small finite quantity of specific data to be performed adequately. Yet, thousands of uncoordinated reports are produced, in varying time periods, sequences, and frequencies, beyond the comprehension and depth at which they can be used effectively.

The overall labor and technology costs of collecting data, formulating it into information, putting it into computers, and storing and retrieving it are increasing exponentially for most companies. It is in the best interest of managers to ensure that the system for providing business knowledge is controlled. This control is much more than installing technology.

To ensure that each business function is synchronized by using only information required to perform it and to ensure that the cost of that same information is minimized, it is necessary to examine the way information relates to strategies and profits. Only if information can always be traced to profits can it be considered essential to the business. The return on investment (ROI) for information is a key consideration.

This chapter describes and exposes various criteria involved in creating a global strategy for accumulating business knowledge.

A STRATEGIC PERCEPTION

Clearly, the highest level of information begins when a company defines (1) missions, (2) objectives, (3) goals, and (4) measurements. The profit-makers of the world spend a great deal of time on these basic subjects because they are the foundation of success in any business venture. Yet, it is probably safe to say that the overwhelming majority of business operatives below the senior management level do not know the difference between these entities and could care less as they struggle with their day-to-day assignments.

The translation of missions, objectives, and goals is frequently not communicated clearly from the boardroom to project levels in the organization. The structure for the translation is missing. To most business operatives, their contact with the company is through information reports or the very fallible verbal interpretation they are given. The relationship of company objectives or goals is most often not translated to any individual's role in meeting the profit expectations of the company.

Many managers have recognized the power that information and communication has on productivity but have not always found a successful means of

1. Conveying meaning
2. Changing perspectives
3. Motivating performance

High-level managers may spend weeks off site in management seminars involving communications, but their staffs never hear what happened or what senior management expects. They are all nice guys but poor communicators with minds of their own.

Translations through many organizational levels frequently result in distortion of tasks relative to the specific goals to be achieved. A key point is that all business operatives must have access to the same goal-related information. As goals are specified, information must be extended to lower levels of related detail. Tightly related nomenclature, content, formats, and time periods to support human efforts are required. If data consistency does not exist, synergy and profits are lost.

In the course of business activities, there is a need to establish direction and guidelines so that the total business can function as a single integrated unit. To establish that direction, company owners, stockholders, and managers have found it necessary to communicate using various high-level information statements. For orientation purposes, this book refers to the highest level of information as mission statements. Missions then encapsulate objectives, and objectives encapsulate goals. How are they related?

Examples of high-level information statements are shown in Box 1.1. They are intentionally divergent to show the lack of coordination that can exist between levels when their subjects are not related.

Unfortunately, Helen, the Accounts Payable Supervisor, has difficulty in understanding how these global statements relate to her daily work. Several levels of interpretation are required, and it is frequently these middle-management translations that ensure sufficient confusion to subvert the intent of senior management. The decision-making process of the organization can become seriously flawed, and profits can fail to materialize. Quick-fix solutions may become part of the corporate culture.

BOX 1.1

High-Level Information Statements

Mission Statements
  Broad ongoing enduring philosophy and direction
- To maintain the highest possible worldwide market
- To keep leadership in the domestic auto industry
- To remain a prime contractor for U.S. military

Objective Statements
  Perceived changes of state to accomplish missions
- To create a highly technical trained work force
- To achieve a high national financial rating
- To become a leader in industrial chemical production

Goal Statements
  Specific planned targets as quantifiable values and time periods to meet objectives
- To increase the technical staff by 20 percent in two years
- To establish a west coast facility this quarter
- To acquire an existing product research organization in six months

---

BOX 1.2

General Business Objectives

Increase	Sales
Develop	New markets
Expand	Market share
Meet	Competition
Improve	Customer service
Improve	Product quality
Contain	Product costs
Increase	Return on investment
Increase	Employee productivity
Clarify	Business rules
Improve	Resource utilization
Improve	Information content
Improve	Communications
Improve	Public image
Meet	Governmental requirements

Many business operatives may have consequently lost touch with what they are doing. They may have lost the "ability to think" how one business subject can affect another because there is no global reference. Information systems clearly reflect any fragmented condition of the business. Knowledge can be lost when it is not properly exposed within the context of the subject to which it belongs. Box 1.2 contains generic examples of objectives which can be applied to most enterprises.

BUSINESS PROFIT MEASUREMENTS

The missions and objectives of a business drive its goals and their associated projects and sequence. The prime result of goals will be plans that directly impact business events, assets, and liabilities. To analyze the impact of goals on plans, projects, and budgets, profit measurement information must be present for each of the selected measurement units of the business.

Box 1.3 is a simple list of commonly used measurements. The accepted sequence of the measurement units is that required for the *profit calculation*. Missions, objectives, and goals must all eventually be related to show their effect on these units. Consequently, measurements are the base upon which all company knowledge and information must focus.

Many businesses establish the specific business measurements and indicators that can best reflect performance, productivity, and resource utilization. All businesses do not have the same set of measurement indicators, but most adhere to similar measurement units.

Several measurement indicators can exist to support the business measurement units:

BUSINESS MEASUREMENT UNIT (BMU)	MEASUREMENT INDICATORS
Sales	Product rate of sale
Purchases	Product cost variances
Inventory	Turnover and storage cost
Manufacturing	Output levels and unit costs
Transport	Shipping volumes and costs

These samples can extend to thousands of combinations of information variables. Most businesses do not control this type of information or analyze its integrated effect on the business overall. The value and use of the measurements are usually left in the hands of accountants rather than departmental managers.

The overall success of a business depends heavily on which measurements and indicators are selected to guide business managers. Once selected, measurements must be maintained and reviewed for consistency and validity.

BOX 1.3

Examples of Business Measurement Unit (BMU)

Business Events	Business Assets	Business Liabilities
Sales	Cash	Payables
Sales costs	Investments	Debts
Manufacturing	Receivables	Stocks
Warehousing	Inventory	Bonds
Distribution	Equipment	Capital
Packaging	Plant	
Transportation	Land	
Gross margin		
Marketing		
Advertising		
Payroll		
Employee benefits		
Communications		
Expenses		
Incomes		
Taxes		
Profits		

Business measurement units describe values.

Unfortunately, the measurement process may be defective, impeding the ability to achieve a goal:

1. Measurements may not be in place.
2. Knowledge may not exist.
3. Business measurements may be flawed.
4. Variance criteria may be undefined.
5. Countervailing relationships may be undefined.

Consider the following examples:

1. An increase in sales may impact product unit costs.
2. Lower product purchase volume may impact inventory and warehouse costs.
3. Purchase frequency may impact customer service levels.

The complexity of the interaction of many entities may severely inhibit the human ability to sort out action steps required to meet business objectives.

An objective such as [increase] [customer service] can be flawed even if the product is a best seller. Business subject integration, described in Chapter 7, facilitates the human ability to examine the relationships and behavior of business entities.

Business knowledge, as it is structured in many companies, is inadequate to satisfy the objective of increasing profits. Fragmented measurements may be in place that provide information only for maximizing the performance of single departments and that cause adverse effects on so many other departments that the total business profits deteriorate. The world of business knowledge, despite the use of computers, has been allowed to become so complex and fragmented that few people can understand the whole. Information itself is not managed well and thereby causes problems that are responsible for lower profits.

The recognition of these current deficiencies (by managers) is a first priority and takes precedence over unchecked computer hardware and software purchases. Information must be organized and directly related to the profit measurements of the business. Meaningful plans and goals depend on these accurate relationships. Knowledge draws it all together if a master platform exists to support a global business review. A purpose of this book is to expose the components of the global platform and the steps to construct it.

If a goal is established, the goal initiator must be able to describe its effect on each of the current profit measurement indicators. If the measurement relationships or subjects are not in place, then it will be impossible to tell if the goal is achievable or what the impact is on the bottom line.

Managers must clearly establish what constitutes a profit and then select the goals required to meet ROI expectations in a projected time period. Creating an integrated knowledge facility to support this process is a major subject of this book.

Linkages between major business subjects can be observed in the following global business rule.

BUSINESS KNOWLEDGE RULE

If

1. Company missions relate clearly to objectives,
2. Objectives tie directly to goals,
3. Goals and plans relate positively to profit measurements, and
4. Profit measurements relate clearly to projects, activities, rules, and subjects,

then

1. Goal ROI can be evaluated.
2. Goals can be properly sequenced.
3. Process productivity can be measured.
4. Profitable performance can be obtained.
5. Information ROI can be determined.

The failure to adequately define and relate knowledge to profits is a major reason that the investment in information systems is yielding a decreasing return to companies. The ROI from information (and its associated computers) is rapidly becoming a major budget concern of U.S. corporate executives, who have noted the following:

The information technology investment is increasing, but the information ROI is decreasing.

The cost of computers is decreasing, while the cost of computer usage is skyrocketing.

The major information relationships that affect the ROI of the business are as follows:

- Information linkage to profit measurements
- Information measurements for the organization of work
- Information coordination for remote locations
- Information about business resources
- Information for transaction control
- Information about products and services

An expanded discussion of these areas may help to clarify how knowledge and its information helps contribute to profits.

> A Management Question: How can we stay competitive and control information costs?

BUSINESS PROCESSES AND RULES

Work Unit Specialization

In any business organization for profit, a clean separation of work processes and their functions and activities has proven to be effective. Business organization units formed around like types of work and a specialization in the division of labor have given rise to productivity, but only up to a point. Many human functions have been converted wholly or partially to computer or robotic functions. This transfer of work has taken place because the cost of a work unit (per time period) was able to be reduced.

In many cases the level of human labor cost can be replaced by lower-labor-cost work units combined with technology units for overall cost reductions across multiple processes.

Automation of Knowledge

Overall automation benefits and job specialization are not achieved without creating offsetting problems. The business rules, calculations, and data are transferred to the computer and, in many cases, promptly forgotten. Human knowledge frequently is dissipated. Highly skilled knowledge workers are often replaced by lower-level, part-time personnel who do not know what is going on inside the machine but only that the buttons work most of the time.

Consequently, higher-cost specialists are required to continually research what the computer is doing and to create more complex changes to the machine work function rules. Carried to its ultimate conclusion, only a few highly skilled knowledge workers may eventually remain who will actually comprehend how the business components relate globally.

Because the computer functions themselves are frequently not organized, each change adds to overall complexity. Every change adds to the time to make subsequent changes. Of course, egos cannot admit that they have lost touch with what the machine is doing. Machine rule documentation is frequently disorganized, fragmented, or lacking altogether. It is no longer a question of *if* the fatal flaws will cause a disaster, only *when*.

Cockpit complacency exists far beyond the realm of aviation. The muddle-on-through philosophy is no longer acceptable.

More computer staff and additional computer hardware are frequently perceived as a substitute for the knowledge gap. This solution is in fact only a temporary stopgap and the long-range impact is higher costs.

The productivity gains achieved by initially transferring human functions to computer functions can be lost in a shift to higher levels of required technical staff expertise.

A factor in the business system evolution has been the steady decrease in costs of computer hardware. Unfortunately, the cost trap of *change* includes more outlays than mere hardware substitution costs. The human errors, time, and training costs related to technological changes and advances add hidden costs and lower productivity to both the technical and business staffs.

The results of many of the new people-computer combinations are a net loss in overall productivity. In spite of much office automation, little productivity has been achieved in 20 years. A new system is frequently a duplicate of what existed previously: a new uniform with little contribution to profit generation capabilities.

The technical staff interest is in technology per se. Their next temporary job is around the corner at another company. This option may not be open to business managers.

One of the fastest growing industries in the United States is the temporary employment agency. Many companies have discovered that specialized skills can be hired on a temporary (no-notice) basis, without incurring costs of benefits, vacations, insurance, illness, or human concern. Substitutable (human) parts will most likely continue to mushroom as a way of corporate life. The offset to this "temp" psychology is a fostering of indifferent attitudes to productivity, boss loyalty, product quality, and the company commitment.

It is difficult to appraise the effect of the ingrained attitude of "take the money and run" on corporate America and its culture. The use of automation has provided a growth environment for both relatively low-skilled "temps" and high-cost knowledge workers. Frequently, mid-level manager jobs are mistakenly forfeited in the cost reduction conversion.

When the above scenario is exploited, the costs of both human and computerized functions are temporarily reduced. Conversely, long-run profit potential must be protected from this uncontrolled computer juggernaut. Increasingly, automation opportunities can be illuminated only with a structured examination of business work function interactions.

A sloppy management of knowledge is a reason why the productivity dilemma exists and continues. Many department managers do not want to be bothered with a structured examination of work decisions. The structuring of work costs time, money, and patience to achieve. It also displays inefficiencies.

Many managers elect to simply react to the problem of the hour. The telephone is always ringing, and a new problem surfaces every minute. Even the "one-minute manager" collapses at 57 seconds. No one person can know or do it all. There are still some managers who have to be involved in every play while their staff is isolated to watch the game unfold. Power islands are maintained at the expense of flexibility. If productivity is lost through the inability to change, then the power cycle may be gradually forfeited.

The reality of the corporate culture is the prime determinant of the quality of business knowledge, its information, and its systems. Corporate culture can be altered positively by the quality and distribution of its information in support of business functions, people, computers, and machines.

Functional Relationships

Organizational structures do not always group related types of work. Typical business processes include the following types, depending on the specific industry:

BUSINESS PROCESSES

Marketing	Human resources
Sales	Engineering
Manufacturing	Product research
Purchasing	Information processing
Warehousing	Finance
Transportation	Accounting

Each business process can be fragmented into hundreds of human activities and computer functions. Each requires knowledge, technology, and people. They are expected to work together to produce a profit.

Every human function and activity

1. Has an associated *cost* of its work unit
2. Requires the definition and maintenance of its rules
3. Requires information to support its decisions
4. Needs to have its performance measured

In any given company, it is not unusual to find over 5000 major human work activities and functions that are undefined. Each function may fragment into hundreds of subtasks that constitute the actual jobs performed. In addition, each computer function requires definition.

As businesses grow, their functions tend to change, overlap, and duplicate. Lines of responsibility tend to become hazy. Information becomes flawed. Decision-makers find they must examine the impact of their actions on all business functions and activities before they act.

In many cases, decisions and actions are committed without regard to their impact on other functions. Then chaos begins. Why? People don't know how to find these relationships. Individual fiefdoms are established. Power politics take hold, and the Chinese walls of organization isolation initiate the destructive process of self-preservation. The preservation of the suborganization becomes the primary objective, superseding and replacing the global return on investment.

Under conditions of increasing competition, the preceding behavior cannot be allowed to exist. If productivity is to be achieved, every function and activity must be examined, measured, and related to its

1. Contribution to profit/cost
2. Duplicity with other functions
3. Support of other functions
4. Replaceability
5. Information needs and rules

When management does not have a simple uniform list of all of the computer functions and human activities in the company, they are seldom able to question interactive cost relationships.

When business functions are not named to reveal what they are or how they relate, then duplications are hidden. Information about the processes, activities, and functions simply may not exist. When these voids occur, costs continue to increase, and profits continue to deteriorate. When managers do not know the *costs* of functions in their department, they cannot be expected to minimize costs.

Information presentation of the costs of functions is a cost itself, which the respective function must absorb. The lack of adequate cost information by function is a major concern of managers seeking an enhancement of productivity. Measurement indicators of functions are required if managers are to know what level of performance they are achieving.

> **Note:** The preceding remarks are about business work processes. Information about business work differs from that which measures the results of business work.

Another type of information that is frequently not controlled or exposed adequately relates to business rules utilized in the execution of the business functions. In any company there can be thousands of business rules that are in place, and used daily, that

1. Clash with countervailing rules
2. Are no longer usable or relevant
3. Are unknown to the staff

These business rules are frequently not organized in any recognizable way. They may be coded into a computer and forgotten until conflicting rules collide. Then, an inordinate expense is required to correct the situation. Information describing business rules must be created and displayed by the organization within which they are used.

When business rules are not created, updated, deleted, or indexed in a structured way, business profits deteriorate in a cluster of errors, corrections, expenses, and legal suits.

In many instances, experienced staff personnel keep rookies advised by word of mouth. This method allows each identical problem to be handled uniquely and repetitively. There is no substitute for a highly structured set of business rules exposing their relationship and sequence of execution.

When a business rule is changed, it can affect hundreds of related rules within computer programs. These relationships simply cannot be remembered by any one person or recalled mentally as changes are implemented, unless they are architected.

Business rule bookkeeping is clearly a computer job. Business rule control and training are essential to maintain and increase business profits. If the enterprise is to survive intense foreign competition, rule identification and its fast access cannot be ignored.

A premise of this book is that all of the described information types must be controlled globally by relating them to their measurement units. This technique is described in Part Two.

A single-tier information schema is needed for the total business. Profits can be dramatically increased by controlling the information of and about the business work processes and their associated business rules in a direct relationship to business measurements. Complex? Yes. Possible? Yes, but only with a global uniform company knowledge architecture.

INFORMATION EFFECTIVENESS

Characteristics

The previous section addressed information about the business processes and functional relationships. When information effectiveness (ROI) is discussed, the information types must be the vehicles used to improve business results.

Information about business performance allows business operatives to adjust their emphasis if it has the following characteristics:

1. The correct content (specific to the results accomplished)
2. The right content level (summary vs. detail)
3. Easy to comprehend (no complex translations required)
4. A high degree of accuracy
5. Fast and easy access (using business terminology)
6. Up-to-date (today's news)
7. Correct time periods and frequencies of occurrence
8. Prompts specific decisions to be made

Frequently, companies have not given adequate attention to this mix in the production of information. Consequently, much of what is produced is not actionable. Profit-making decisions may not take place at the right time. The information ROI is then low.

There are several reasons why much of the information about business results does not result in overall productivity. They relate to people, rapid changes, and limited planning.

The technological *how to* produce information frequently preempts the *what* and *why* certain knowledge is required. Hardware selection can take precedence over information selection. If information is to facilitate action, then it must be available in the right content and context, at the right place, at the right time. Computer hardware is only a mechanism. Knowledge should be its master. Information productivity must be related to profits.

> Profits evolve from information when
> 1. Accuracy and speed prevail
> 2. Interpretation is clear and simple
> 3. No translations are required
> 4. A global context exists

Interpretation

When information is developed and technology is directed at only selected business processes, the prime goal is frequently to reduce functional costs. The information produced is primarily directed to support a unique part of the business.

Management in one area of the business simply may not see how other business area information is significant to their activities. Consequently, data developed in one business unit is not always consistent with that of another area of the business. The format, values, time periods, detail data levels, updating frequency, and nomenclature present so many variations that interpretation becomes complex. Standardization across the company becomes almost impossible.

Multiple names are frequently applied to identical business information measurements. Subjects can mean one thing to one department and another thing to another department. The actions that managers take based on their reports frequently become counterproductive to their peers. One of the results of this diversity is hundreds of meeting hours just to gain a common understanding of the facts.

Common business terminology and nomenclature make a big difference in people's ability to interpret facts accurately and then to work together. Without common business terminology as a base, more information volume becomes counterproductive.

Technical staffs frequently proliferate codes to the point where it is impossible to explain what the information is or why it exists. Governmental and military nomenclatures are examples of the compression of long phrases to acronyms interpretable by only a select few.

The comparison of operational information to a plan or to standards is crucial to performance measurement. Traditionally, if managers are allowed to select their own acronyms and measurements, they choose elements that most favorably reflect on local performance. If managers are not directly involved in measurement standards, it may be very difficult to obtain a consistent view of the global business performance.

The classic example is the production line experiencing abnormally high setup costs. Work is adjusted to meet the way the orders arrive. The Production Department is unable to perceive that the Sales Department is causing increased costs by the way it is taking orders.

Interpretation requires interlocking information, measurements, and simplicity. The highest levels of reporting must be able to be linked and related to the lowest level of detail reporting for the same subject or relationships between subjects.

Interrelated departmental information is required for group productivity. Otherwise, each department only thinks of optimizing its own productivity no matter how unproductive some actions may be for all other departments. "We did our job" is a group-defeating default.

> Global information can increase productivity between departments when it is uniformly interpreted. Information interpretation incurs costs and requires
> 1. Structured nomenclature
> 2. Simplicity
> 3. Clarity
> 4. Training

Accuracy/Availability

Frequently, computer technology has been applied to helping front-line people perform their functional jobs better. Significant strides have been made in transaction automation. Terminals of every kind assist and control business operatives in day-do-day transaction recording. This type of automation has greatly contributed to the accuracy of the data that describes what happened, where it happened, and who was responsible.

One of the major problems confronting many companies is that data collected soon becomes lost in computerized data banks where it is not available for a period of time, too long to allow action.

Although computer file access enables a company to be more accurate in immediate customer service, the time lags, processing stages, and information accessibility may not allow business profits to materialize. Sequential operations must give way to simultaneous operations. Volumes of reports continue to pile up and are thrown out because they are useless and too voluminous.

Operating managers frequently ask, "Why do they keep giving me all of this paper?" The confusion goes on costing businesses thousands of otherwise profit dollars. The speed and accuracy of the data collection may be adequate, but the usability of it all is marginal.

Information can be used for profit-making decisions if it is accurately captured as it occurs: correlated, reduced, and analyzed on a day-to-day basis. This does not preclude the need to examine long-term trends but does require the establishment of relationship rules of key data. These relationships are described in Chapter 4.

Business operatives are frequently so engrossed in getting the numbers to balance from one report to another that any attention to the customer, the vendor, the service, or the product quality is purely coincidental.

Business operatives must be alerted to what information exists and is available to them. Profits evolve
from information when
1. Data is easily accessible
2. Summary levels of information exist
3. Responsibility and accountability
   for information content exist

Communication

The lack of human communication is yet another reason why profits
fail to materialize. Of course, there are instances where no action takes
place even when information is transmitted and acknowledged twice. This
is probably due to the fact that both action and the lack of action are not
required to be reported.

Some people search for information, but most fail to pass it on. The
enemy is the assumption that the word is passed and that one person
communicates with the same effectiveness as another. Even when the
problems of nomenclature, format, accuracy, and availability of information are overcome, people are not

1. Fast in interpreting
2. Long on remembering
3. Perceptive in communicating

What action should be taken? Human memories are short. Knowledge
must be retained in a way that it can be commmunicated quickly.

The boil-up process in some companies can take forever or just not
happen at all. This is frequently due to the lack of multiple channels with
which to broadcast significant business events. People learn by both impact
and repetition; some never learn, and very few learn to communicate
effectively. The basic blocking and tackling of communication has been
neglected in many companies despite outrageous expenditures for data
processing devices. "Everyone knows that" is assumed and can produce
disastrous results. The expression [cubicle, sweet cubicle] implies the
isolation of many corporate departments.

The best information systems in the world are no better than the
people using them. One hand may not know what the other is doing. Some
managers may not want information distributed because they feel their
power base will be upset. "I've got a secret" has no place in a business
venture. More time can be spent defending a position or an ego than
activating profitable action between departments of the business based on
facts. The question is, What can be done about this dilemma?

Most people want to do a good job and be rewarded for it. They must be provided with information and freedom to learn how their job fits and interacts with the product quality and profits of the company. Management improves performance by providing the communication environment with free-flowing information about events, performance, and rules. Some managers want the secrets kept under the rug, especially the bad news. The penalty for a press release (complaint) is termination. If you like your job, pay, and security, keep quiet. Modify poor results to look good even if their exposure is what the company urgently needs. To overcome this defeating behavior, managers must insist on having a facility to view the information of other managers. Then communication takes place quickly. Isolated information inhibits communication. Peer networks are the future. They cannot exist without a common business architecture and a physical facility to access related information.

Management needs to expose the linkage between information and profits. Profits evolve from information when

1. Business measurements have decision criteria displayed directly with the information
2. The action taken is displayed directly with the information that prompts it
3. Business rules associated with the action are displayed directly with the information
4. Management reviews decisions and rules and the actions taken

---

Management Mandate

In most companies, the information needed exists somewhere. The challenge is to put it together in a consistent framework of relationships and to train managers to use it.

Information does not automatically mean profits when it is not accessible, when it is too voluminous to make sense, or when the management mandate for problem exposure does not exist.

Managers are the only ones who can set the climate for profit making through information exposure, dispersion, and prescribed action.

The behavior of all people in a company is highly dependent on the information they receive. It is clear that management must have the methodology and tools to establish a common information base. If the distribution of information is to take place, a common format and architecture is needed for data. With a common architecture, every aspect of the business activity can be regularly, clearly, and consistently reviewed.

All of the latest technology, computer systems, local area networks, personal computers, data bases, word processors, and technologies cannot substitute for architected knowledge. Major outlays for technology without a structure for the total company information is ludicrous.

Layers of middle-management translators add to administrative overhead as a substitute for information structure. Fortunately for many companies, their competitors are in the same state of disarray. The stockholders are far enough removed to be unaware of the negative effect of information disarray.

Managers are safe until their competition creates an integrated knowledge structure.

In some companies an emphasis has been placed on automating and controlling the flow of transactions and producing financial reports. When the numbers come up short, the money-counters have often been the first to direct action because the nonfinancial operatives do not have adequate work/rule information to suggest alternate courses of action.

"Cut costs" may be the only perceived direction. However, more outlays for service, product quality, or knowledge may be better long-range solutions. Operating departments must frequently use accounting reports to evaluate what is needed.

Few accounting reports accumulate and store knowledge about what business rules work and what business rules do not work under specific conditions. As the business expands and contracts, the information produced continues to be after the fact. If action does take place, it is frequently too little/too late. Few operational reports bridge the relationships between the operating departments so that one can synchronize with another for overall productivity.

Business action cannot translate into profits when the nonfinancial operatives (marketing, purchasing, manufacturing, warehousing, customer service) are not synchronized by broad and interactive rules. It is to this knowledge integration and automated expertise that the computer systems of the future must be directed.

Many knowledge coordinating systems are currently in their embryonic stages. Primarily, they address specific scientific, medical, or engineering problems that draw upon expert decisions and experience rules.

Management can take a proactive role in preparing for knowledge systems by insisting on clear rules and architected information. These rules are not addressed by *managing by wandering around* (MBWA). What is learned must be accumulated into an architected framework of transferable and accessible knowledge.

This effort requires tough, meticulous analysis. Information produces profits when it provides a business operative with the opportunity to move one more inch in achieving quality performance. Each businesss operative must be exposed to the knowledge required to execute his or her job.

Knowledge can facilitate or inhibit
- Profit increases
- Cost reductions

THE USE OF TECHNOLOGY

If the knowledge and information cost to support a business is more than the added value that the activity can earn using it, should it be created at all?

Frequently, companies produce so much scrap data in a day that the entire staff of the company cannot read, yet analyze it, in a month. This excess waste can be found in most data processing departments under the guise that the accountants/auditors may want to see this detail at some future time. The future never comes. In fact, auditors may want to examine samples of detail, but not on a daily basis.

People cannot utilize volumes of data. Costly volume excesses dramatically reduce business profits. The computers of many companies work three shifts to sort and rearrange data six ways to Sunday because certain individuals seek a safety blanket in detail.

Finding and eliminating excess information are no less important than finding the duplicate human functions previously discussed. For those intent on reducing costs of the business, data processing itself has become one of the most fertile areas. The tendency within data processing is to leave whatever is running and add on new systems, ignoring any redundancies that may be created.

Frequently, new hardware or packages are installed only to result in close replicas of the previous system. Because of the disjointed way computer programs have been laced together, the rework required to eliminate this duplication could cost more than the savings that can be achieved: a real catch 22! Old systems and programs seem to never die. They keep running long after they are useless because it is perceived to be too difficult to find and eliminate them.

An examination of the major cost centers of business technology can clarify how these excesses can be identified. What are these mechanized cost centers?

Information Storage Is a Major Cost Center

Information storage technology is decreasing in the cost per data unit stored, but the total cost of the storage function and its associated technical activity may offset this advantage in many instances.

Technical issues concerning *where* to store information (centralization vs. decentralization) frequently precede the more important consideration of *what* and *how much* should be stored.

Due to the already heavy investment in computerized files, there are those who now suggest that a master directory is all that is needed to reference the locations of existing data, wherever it is. Then all business operatives can have open access to it while using multiple applications, hardware, software, and network protocols.

Major companies have fallen for this oversimplified high-cost technical solution to a problem that need not exist. It can keep high-salaried technicians busy for years.

Still other companies believe in distributing information but not in having distributed information storage facilities. Frequently, information is jammed into a central all-inclusive file to allow, theoretically, any number of business operatives to access it as a centrally shared resource. Frequently, business users wait due to slow computer response times. Waiting for work is a costly business function seldom exposed by business managers.

In many cases, the demand for file access is simply too great to allow anyone enough time to find what they are seeking. Luckily, the computer times them out. Software and hardware companies are promising more effective "technical solutions" to what amounts to an information management problem.

The central fact is that a major cost of a business is its files of disjointed information, which can become the nemesis of business profits. The key to control of this hidden cost center lies in the naming and indexing of the information content itself.

For example, can purchase-receiving history stored on line for the previous five years be justified? Where managers are not accountable for the cost of their information, the perception can be that it is free.

Information Collection Is a Major Cost Center

Some of the most impressive technical achievements have been made in data collection devices, for example,

Video display terminals (VDTs)	Product code scanners/labels
Video text displays	Personal ID entry pads
Automatic teller machines (ATMs)	Communication networks

These devices and their related software have greatly facilitated the recording, control, editing, validating, and transmission of business transactions. These controllers of human and machine interaction have enabled the unit cost of transactions to decrease dramatically. In addition, data integrity, customer service, training, accuracy, and speed have been enhanced. Many of these features have been utilized since the early 1970s.

However, the total cost is increasing because of a greater quantity and variations in the content collected. The myth of this accelerated growth in data collection is that it appears incrementally cheaper to collect data. It is easy to ask the computer to perform a thousand hours of data collection to find out more and more about less and less. The perception that the terminal and computer are free has prevailed. Gathering more data seems defensible.

If being able to find out if a proposed airline flight has a gum dispenser aboard actually results in one additional ticket sale, who can argue with that? The incremental cost of data collection seems inconsequential. Eventually, incremental collections can become prohibitive. A finite number of human tasks required to enter a transaction is reached.

Superfluous data recording costs hard dollars, and it is a major business excess. With more demand for real-time data entry, even for accounting journal entries, the cost of information recording can be expected to parallel the cost of labor.

Data terminal hardware costs are decreasing, but the total network payroll cost of collecting data is increasing due to volume, variety, and staff wages.

Information collection has become a major cost center requiring controls and cost measurements.

Information Validation Is a Major Cost Center

The increased editing and validation of business transactions by computer have significantly increased. What used to be referenced as "garbage in" has, at minimum, become "accurate garbage in." It has been approximated that 30 percent of all computer processing is applied to edit/validation functions.

There is little argument against the advantage of accurate information. The techniques of using check digits suffixed to control identification numbers protect many people from receiving their neighbors' bills, a wrong bank statement, or a wrong item from a catalog house because of a data entry clerk error.

Validations (comparing data to existing reference files) contribute to business transaction accuracy in a way impossible in the 1960s, because computer speed and file access have dramatically improved.

There is, however, a hidden cost factor of maintaining voluminous dedicated lists and files to a high level of accuracy so that every business transaction can be fully edited and validated. People have to control lists and tables against which the transaction is validated. The more detail included in the business transactions, the more human control costs are required to ensure the validation criteria are correct.

Another control problem inherent in many business computer programs is that historically programmers could not trust their data. In many programs that process transactions sequentially, each program may reexecute the same edit/validate functions as its predecessor.

Management seldom inspects this level of detail, which can incur significant costs. While the hardware cost to edit and validate business transactions is decreasing, the total cost to control this function can be increasing. This author's experience is that 10 to 15 percent of computer costs are incurred in editing and validating data. The exact percentage of computer processing costs incurred in editing and validation is subjective; however, the real costs can be substantial. This cost makes validation a major cost center worth controlling.

A way to help control edit/validation costs lies in the standardized naming of computer program modules so that duplications by type of validation can be exposed.

Information Updating Is a Major Cost Center

A single business transaction, even using the most prevalent type of file structures, may not update one time but several times in a system. A single sales order transaction may post a sales file, a customer file, an inventory file, a transport file, a vendor file, a purchase order file, and a general ledger file.

In many businesses, these files are kept and maintained as separate entities. In some cases, these complex sets of files are passed for updating daily, weekly, or monthly. The associated controls to post this separation of files mean added human costs to ensure that all of the files are available, accurate, and in balance.

When the updating is not accomplished concurrently in the same time instance, data processing costs remain higher than the alternative of one time posting. Various programs add to the complexity by accumulating information in uncoordinated time periods to satisfy specialized accumulations and summaries (week-to-date, month-to-date, quarter-to-date, year-to-date, previous/current year, etc.).

The updating and summary accumulation of information can be very disjointed. When program logic changes are required, many chains of related programs must be adjusted. Keeping track of all of these changes frequently does not take place.

New programmers begin to mangle the work of their predecessors. Time pressures and the lack of methodical documentation take their toll in each successive change. The rewrite of updating code is a continuing cost.

Additional costs are incurred because of the need to back up copy files in case of operational errors, hardware failures, and programmer errors.

Protected reusable building block code is the exception rather than the rule despite the cost advantages that could be obtained.

Why do these ad hoc methods continue? It is because they are perceived as merely technical problems and are ignored by business managers as a cost center to be managed.

Information Manipulation Is a Major Cost Center

After incoming business transactions have updated a full set of business files, programs are applied to manipulate data content. The human cost to control this file manipulation can become excessive if the computer rules are not documented or are changed haphazardly. Frequently, computer programs are in a continuous state of disarray.

As an increasing number of business departments seek to utilize the same files, an increasing number of programs manipulate the contents of the same files. In some businesses where files are kept on separate computers (PCs-mini-hosts), the contention for the same information creates confusion and differing results.

The manipulation of business information on separately controlled computers can add materially to human costs of verifying the overall accuracy and consistency of the system.

The computer hardware cost per unit of instruction is decreasing, but an added number of detail manipulations can increase the human handling costs.

It is not unusual to find computer programs that calculate identical information but fail to record it for other programs to use. A misconception is that repetitive recalculation is always less expensive than the storage of its result. Consequently, thousands of program modules can calculate duplicate data that, undocumented, escapes detection. Because data is not identified, it is not accessible and is difficult to detect.

An emphasis must be placed on how to identify data, what the data means, and where duplicate data is created.

Information Reporting Is a Major Cost Center

Remarkable technological strides have been made in information displays. What used to be available only in printed formats is now available in color graphics and animated figures supplemented by easy user menus that require little computer knowledge to use. Conversational interaction with computer questions is no longer a confusing pattern of sign-on codes. Voice-activated terminals will soon enable more people than ever before to access and correspond through the computer.

As in the previously described cost centers, the unit cost of information display hardware is decreasing; however, the increase in the total display cost is caused by an uncontrolled demand and the technological ease of use. The perception is easy to develop that information displays are free. If the computer and the terminal devices are installed and everyone has access to even a small part of the total, the combined time to "play with it" will dramatically increase costs.

If managers do not begin to exercise control of the information content requests and the frequency of accesses, the computer can be turned loose, exercising thousands of hours of computer time to obtain useless, nonactionable reports.

Information overload already exists. It is not unusual for even experienced programmers to burn up hours of computer time testing against full files and to dump boxes of useless paper printouts for a simple program test. After all, they don't pay the bills, and no one reports them. It's part of the art.

Many current computer programs perform transaction control, edit/validation, updating, file management, manipulation, and information display functions in one large set of logic. Traditionally, the argument was directed to saving computer file access time. This argument might have been validated if no changes were ever necessary. However, the complexity that is created by combining all functions, but the kitchen sink, in one large program creates kludges that eventually produce chaos when changes are needed.

Additional costs are incurred to pump hundreds of information displays over communication lines to remote sites. In some cases, entire files are transmitted to remote sites so that anyone can look at what is stored by a remote computer.

> Work expands to fit the information available (an extension of Parkinson's Law).

SUMMARY

This chapter broadly describes why and how business knowledge and information can affect business profits and costs. More technology frequently contributes little more to business profits than its predecessors. Functional costs may decrease in one business area but increase in another, because integrated data planning (global vision) does not exist.

Various deficiencies exist in information itself. Although unique system costs can be reduced, only an investment in a unified and integrated knowledge structure and related tools can facilitate a higher level of productivity.

The emphasis in this book is on a rather simple *strategy* needed to join and integrate all business subjects. Its purpose is to create and maintain a uniform knowledge shell about work, rules, and information accessible by all business managers.

There are those who believe today's business managers lack the will

1. To pursue knowledge engineering
2. To understand its effect on profit generation
3. To install the disciplines that it provokes

In fact, the leaders of most new businesses have been more than able to pursue the torture of thought that knowledge engineering invokes. Why this is true may be the most important aspect of this book. They have been able to quickly grasp the connection between business events and entities.

Part Two describes how business entity relationships can be created for and accessed by managers. Part Three describes how an organization can implement tools for managers in order to unify their environment.

Business knowledge automation has been an evolution involving four stages:

1. *Data*: pieces of related facts and their values
2. *Information*: entity relationship binding to formulate context
3. *Knowledge*: information relationship binding to business rules to formulate expertise
4. *Judgment*: knowledge binding in a global context to expose profitable rules

Historically, the use of computers has been at stage 1, *data* processing. This stage primarily addresses the manipulation of pieces of data for subsequent human analysis.

As business computerization proceeds, the ascending stages concentrate on the interaction of the pieces of data to form information. It simply takes too long for any employee to learn the whole business and to repeatedly decide what information needs to be associated, even if the background of the puzzle (missions, objectives, goals) is well defined. Even the most experienced lose their place. The puzzle is too complex. The cost of (trial and error) training is too high.

New pioneers have recently embarked on the stage 3 level of *knowledge* under the acronym of *artificial intelligence*. The joining of information with many expert rules preserves that which has been learned. This type of knowledge involves complex definitions and procedures controlled by software.

The success of more advanced techniques relies heavily on

1. The architected presentation of information
2. The correctness of the knowledge rules applied to that information
3. A consistent information view for business managers

Future generations may look back in amazement at the lack of information and rule architecture coordination in today's business ventures. Spreadsheets without automated decision rules or help action screens will be a thing of the past.

When business managers finally decide to create and control their knowledge base in addition to their data base, their competitive ability will increase.

How business knowledge can be constructed in a *global* context is a principal subject of Part Two. The manager may initially ask, "Is it even possible to construct a global business knowledge architecture?" (Chapters 4–7).

Prior to describing *how to*, it is first appropriate to ask *what* is the global scope of the information to be organized and *who* is responsible for the effort (Chapters 2 and 3).

Business profits can only be achieved when business managers are sufficiently motivated to demand work tools to construct knowledge. It is clear that motivation is not imposed or delegated. Motivation develops when the perspective of managers is enlarged so they can envision their own membership in the global enterprise. Automated knowledge structures support that vision by allowing any business entity to be quickly associated with any other business entity.

The business work productivity and knowledge quality relationship is depicted in Figure 1.1.

FIGURE 1.1 Business knowledge and work productivity. (a) Using architected information; (b) Using non-architected information.

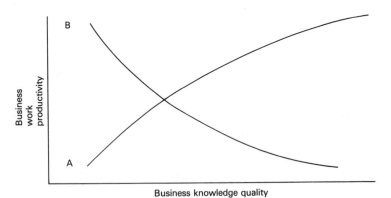

Business knowledge quality

Chapter 2

The Scope of Business Knowledge

INTRODUCTION

The scope of business knowledge appears so extensive that most people do not believe that a knowledge model for an entire business organization can exist.

Many companies specialize in gathering specific types of information about business subjects for resale to others. These companies have developed data bases for unique subjects that can be updated, indexed, associated, and retrieved.

Business information usually revolves around isolated subjects such as markets, companies, customers, vendors, products, services, governmental regulations, and legal references. The computerization of information has made it possible to store vast quantities of detail in separate lists and files. To find a specific instance, a key word or its number is used. If the file or table of subjects is in a sequence, some order is achieved.

Seemingly, the whole world works with its indexed and sequenced files. What, then, causes all of the problems and costs associated with business information? It is the fact that subjects do not stand alone but rather relate in many combinations of subjects in a variety of ways.

People do not think or work one subject at a time. Yet, that is the way many computer subjects have been programmed. The time lapse required to put together relational significance can cause humans to forget the reason why information is sought.

Even with two files of separately sequenced subjects, some people have correlation problems. When the associations reach to three, five, seven, or more relationships, people cannot cope with the extensive thought process. Yet, the computer can maintain any number of subject relationships.

Knowledge has begun to grow in complexity and is no longer adequate as a display of separate subjects. The term *information integration* is used to denote combinations of related subjects.

In addition to the data association problem, people have traditionally used their own words (synonyms) for identical meanings and expressions. Identical files are created using different words. The part file, the item file, the product file, and the material file can be created separately for the same identical information because of personal naming preferences of their creators. Different file names for identical subjects are allowed to accommodate individual preferences.

This duplicity depends on the industry terminology and the personal backgrounds and restrictions of various computer hardware and software vendors. Computer vendors have also created new words and languages to keep their own nomenclature organized. This discipline is imposed on the company choosing their products.

The results to date can keep technicians busy for years with translations and protocols to and from various hardware and software. The number of fourth- and fifth-generation languages, yet to be contrived, defies the imagination. Every new computer language and its hardware dissipate the limited talent available to grapple with these idiosyncrasies. The cost of this turmoil materially detracts from company profits.

To cope with the preceding scenario, it is necessary for a business to organize its information and functions for every aspect of the enterprise. This organization usually takes the form of business and information models.

With the right information model, it is possible to examine business processes, transactions, files, reports, and business rules and to display incongruencies that exist. If information is never organized, it will always appear that more data is required. Standard nomenclature is clearly a first step.

Most companies do not have information models or metaphors to relate the total business. Few have even a standard business dictionary. Precision has not been a universal trait in American business. To understand the total scope of company business, it is necessary to classify subjects and pursue the relationships between them. Agnosia (the failure to recognize objects) frequently prevails in American business.

BUSINESS INFORMATION SCOPE

The scope of business information is frequently unique to specific industries and companies within them. However, there are certain information subjects that establish a generic base, common to all. Each of these subjects has subelements; the following information classifications help to illustrate business information scope.

Business Measurements

Business measurement units were displayed in Chapter 1. Box 1.3 listed measurements that are the major events, assets, and liabilities of the business. For example, sales, purchases, inventory, and transportation are unique major subjects that sequence and quantify the highest classification of business information.

Every business constructs its own set of measurements, but they follow the same overall sequence. Measurements can be extended to lower levels of event significance, for example,

SALES	PURCHASES	INVENTORY
Sales__costs	Purchase__costs	Inventory__products
Sales__returns	Purchase__returns	Inventory__models
Sales__commissions	Purchase__allowances	Inventory__assemblies
Sales__discounts	Purchase__discounts	Inventory__parts

The business measurement classification of information is the nucleus of control for most businesses. Although many companies choose to operate only by the values of the measurement subjects, some have fallen to competitiors when they failed to focus on lower-level subjects such as customers, vendors, products, and employees. Chapter 4 describes how all business subjects can be arranged in a global hierarchy of levels and relationships.

Business Organizations

Business organization units can frequently change for a variety of reasons. The responsibility for the various business units of the company can be clear or hazy but are closely dependent on the relationships and direction of management. The information needed by an enterprise is dependent on precise definitions of its business units and their relationships.

In some companies, internal organization definitions are clear and precise. In other companies, some units defy their reason for existence. Figure 2.1 is a sample hierarchical view of some internal business organi-

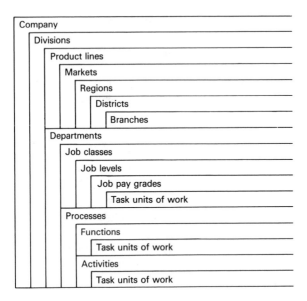

FIGURE 2.1   Business organization unit relationships, company work encapsulation (sample). Each internal business organization unit can consist of lower-level organizational units. Types of organization relationships are not identical for all companies; however, they must be uniquely defined and then consistently used.

zation relationships. It is clear that the sample business organization units can consist of lower-level organization units and can be viewed independently from the way a company responsibility is assigned.

Business organization relationships are totally within the control of the company. How they are named, defined, and associated will affect the organization of information to support them. Each business enterprise must define how its organizations relate.

It is clear that business organization units can extend the meaning of the major measurement subjects previously described. Note the following example of a critical set of relationships:

BUSINESS MEASUREMENT UNIT	(BY)	BUSINESS ORGANIZATION UNIT
Sales	by	Company
Purchases	by	Division
Inventory	by	Product line
Transportation	by	Department
Payroll	by	Function

Any enterprise must clearly establish its business measurements and its organization units. Connections must then be established between these entity types where the information about the relationships is critical to the success of the business. These relationships will be unique by company.

Business Locations

Business units clearly can have many physical locations. The business events that take place at multiple locations frequently require like information to be reported for each site. Events that occur at one site can affect what should occur at another. Multiple sites extend the volume of information needs to still another dimension.

Figure 2.2 is a hierarchical view of physical-location-type relationships that businesses must define and associate. Each of these location types can embrace lower-level locations. They frequently require extensive numbering systems, which are costly to maintain. When locations change, they can affect a sizable number of data permutations. The cost of these changes can be significant.

The number of extensions of subject relationships in the information spectrum caused by location variations is worth observing. For example, note the following:

BUSINESS MEASUREMENT	(BY)	INTERNAL UNIT	(BY)	LOCATION
Sales	by	Division	by	State
Purchases	by	Department	by	City
Inventory	by	Product line	by	Bin number

Business managers must ultimately select the detail of information to be carried that makes sense. The cost to support company information at a location level of detail can be very high.

The information levels required must be selected when the business knowledge project is implemented. Chapter 8 describes the knowledge project implementation plan.

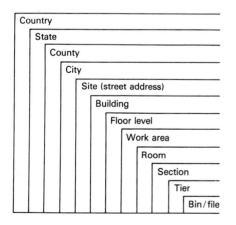

Country
State
County
City
Site (street address)
Building
Floor level
Work area
Room
Section
Tier
Bin / file

FIGURE 2.2 Business location units, internal company location encapsulation (sample). Each geographical/political/physical location consists of encapsulated smaller unit levels until the smallest physical space has been identified and defined. The location units will be used to consistently define where the company events take place and where the company assets are located.

Distribution Channels

Many companies have various channels for product distribution. These channels depend on the type of company products, customers, and services that need to be provided, for example,

Agents	Distributors
Licensees	Brokers
Dealers	Governments
Customers	Wholesalers
Retailers	Franchises

The distribution channel can have multiple information requirements depending on the contractual agreements concerning product quality, service levels and priorities, delivery and distribution methods, invoicing, payments, price breaks, and packaging.

The distribution category of subjects is only *partially* within the control of the company. However, distribution classifications have many parameters in common.

Information is maintained at both the distribution category level as well as the indiviual customer level. Clearly, the business rules to accommodate the marketing channel variances between customers can be significant. The integration chain of customer information can be extended and coupled using the previous classification sequence, for example,

MEASUREMENT	(BY)	ORGANIZATION	(BY)	LOCATION	(BY)	DISTRIBUTION
Sales	by	Product line	by	City	by	Agent
Transport	by	Region	by	Building	by	Consumer

Businesses must concisely define the extent of distribution channel alliances for which information must be maintained. When the strings of information become too long, productivity measurement is more complex. Information becomes excessive when its cost does not yield the incremental return on investment compared with any other business investment.

Procurement Channels

Many companies have various channels of product procurement. These classes can depend on the types of product and service purchases required in the course of manufacturing or distributing materials for resale, for example,

Product vendors	Consultants
Service vendors	Contractors
Supply vendors	Banks
Manufacturers	Insurers
Packagers	Auditors

The procurement channels can have different information requirements depending on contractural agreements concerning product quality, service levels and priorities, delivery/transport methods, invoicing, payments, price breaks, and packaging.

The procurement subjects are only *partially* within the control of the company. However, vendors have many parameters in common that require tracking.

Information is frequently maintained at the procurement class level as well as for the individual vendor level. The business rules to accommodate the channel variances between vendors can be significant. Like the distribution class, the integration chain of vendor information can be extended using the previous classifications, for example,

MEASUREMENT	(BY)	ORGANIZATION	(BY)	LOCATION	(BY)	PROCUREMENT
Purchases	by	Department	by	City	by	Contractor
Transport	by	Division	by	State	by	Carrier

Companies must define their own procurement channel alliances. When the strings of information become too long, productivity measurement is more complex. Information costs must be compared to alternative investments to determine their true worth. Information cost centers were identified in Chapter 1.

Product Classifications

Many companies have various classes of products. These classes can relate to the market, distribution, and procurement channels that exist for buying, selling, or servicing these products. Products can have many levels of encapsulation, for example,

```
Product_class
     Product_model
          Product_unit
               Product_assemblies
                    Product_parts
                         Product_part_properties
```

The product information requirements can extend to many services that support the product such as service agreements, guarantees, and warranties. Many product properties, such as the cost of raw materials, may be beyond the control of the company. Information must frequently be maintained for all levels of support for its products and services.

The maintenance function for updating product records is a major cost of most businesses. The relationship of products to customers, vendors, and competitors is significant. Many ancillary relationships must be maintained, such as bills of material, drawings, catalogs, etc.

One of the key questions is whether the product contributes to or detracts from the company profit. Profit by product is one of the most illusive pieces of business information. The product mix can frequently shield product losers right up to the point of company bankruptcy. Product profitability exposure can be facilitated when the product and all of its relationships are consistently tracked and reviewed.

For all of the preceding reasons, the levels at which the company classifies its product are critical to the knowledge of the business. Product extensions and relationships to major business subjects must be carefully identified, for example,

MEASUREMENT	(BY)	ORGANIZATION	(BY)	LOCATION	(BY)	PRODUCT
Sales	by	Market	by	State	by	Product
Purchases	by	Division	by	City	by	Assembly
Inventory	by	Department	by	Area	by	Part

Each company must identify its unique product properties and their relationships to the previously described subject categories.

The critical subject relationships determine the scope of what information must be carried. Chapter 4 describes a method for structuring the selected product information.

Employee Classifications

The employees of a company are usually classified in reference to the level and type of work performed. Job classes relate closely to processes, activities, and functions previously described, which in turn relate to the measurement units of payroll and benefits.

Clearly, the employee job classification can have many levels in its integration chain, for example,

    Employee job class
        Senior management
        Middle management
        Technical management
        Administration
        Operational

The extensions that can apply to the employee job class must be related as in the previous examples:

MEASUREMENT	(BY)	ORGANIZATION	(BY)	LOCATION	(BY)	JOB CLASS
Payroll	by	Company	by	Country	by	Management
Payroll	by	Division	by	State	by	Operations
Payroll	by	Department	by	City	by	Technical
Payroll	by	Department	by	City	by	Exempt

Employee classes are easily confused with job titles and business processes. It is important to establish unique names for employee classes and then to appraise the extension information strings that are required to manage the human resource.

Employee job classes can be extended by job types such as the following:

Buyers	Programmers	Clerks	Accountants
Secretaries	Analysts	Planners	Laborers

The number of permutations that are necessary to factor and measure variations can become meaningless and costly where they are not controlled.

A major purpose of standard job class/type structures is to control required staff skills and their costs. Chapter 4 describes an example of the employee subject structure.

Environmental Classifications

Environmental classifications consist of all of those factors that are beyond the control of the company. The following list is an abbreviated set of environmental subjects about which a business may elect to maintain information:

Economic classifications
    Gross national product statistics
    Business news
    Money market data
    Currency values
    Interest rates
    Money supply
    Investment alternatives
    Security quotes

Governmental factors
    Budgets
    Tax laws
    Employment laws
    Safety laws
    Labor laws
    Advertising controls

Competitive factors
    Commodity costs
    Labor costs
    Technology costs
    Product types/prices
    Market profiles/lists
    Vendor sources
    Credit data
    Company appraisals

Some of these classes may critically affect decisions regarding previously described classes. It is important to have the ability to relate their impact on the business measurements.

Several levels of environmental factors may affect each other and impact profits of the company. Environmental factors tend to be maintained at very high levels for strategic planning purposes, but it is information that belongs in the information inventory. Each company must carefully select which environmental factors are needed to track environmental subjects. Many business subjects are not environmental information dependent; however, this classification can be expected to become more important as public data bases grow.

Some businesses use complex econometric models to track leading indicators as they relate to their products. Other businesses simply carry organized fact lists to expose external influences that can affect their industry. In any case, environmental information is an important part of the overall business information spectrum.

Business Process Types

Information about company work involves all of the internal functions of the company. Business processes are high-level groups of related types of work. The work types tend to remain relatively stable, even when organizational responsibilities change.

Box 2.1 is a sample of high-level business process names. There can be many others. Each of the business processes can fragment into smaller units of work that must be defined at even lower levels of detail.

Most business process information will consist of how the job is to be performed and how much each job costs per unit of output. For purposes of definition, subsequent chapters will define the separation of labor as follows:

1. Business functions
   Physical types of repetitive work tasks
   Producing business transactions
   Using static rules

2. Business activities
   Mental types of nonrepetitive analysis/planning
   Requiring business knowledge/information
   Using flexible rules

Where duplicate work functions or activities exist, their elimination and automation (or combination) are keys to lower costs, higher productivity, and more profits. Where human work functions can be transposed to or facilitated by technological functions, performance gains are usually achieved. Where human activities can be transferred to or facilitated by computer/machine functions, productivity increases are usually achieved.

When new systems are proposed, their effect on business functions and activity costs is a prime consideration.

BOX 2.1

Business Processes		
Marketing	Manufacturing	Purchasing
Inventory control	Transportation	Human resources
Information	Financial	Research/engineering

When a company fails to concentrate on business functions, inefficiencies and higher costs usually begin. Businesses may spend much more time on debt, takeovers, or financial market casinos than on their own products. The focus of attention on work types is frequently responsible for cost improvements.

When all of the business work functions are named and documented in their *sequence* of execution, the result is called a business model. A system flow chart is another view of this sequence of functions.

Questions that arise concerning the business processes include the following:

Are all of the work functions and activities defined and adequately named?
What is the cost of these functions and activities?
Are any functions or activities duplicated or not needed?
What is the measurement information needed for each of the functions?
Will technology decrease or increase functional cost?
Can information improve the quality or speed of decisions and actions?

The sequence and interaction of all of the work functions must be defined prior to the application of any technology. If the functional relationships and integration of work are not clear, then premature computerization can create added control problems and costs for those functions not involved in the automation cycle.

Business Rule Classification

Perhaps the most important knowledge classification is the business rule. A business rule can be very simple or incredibly complex. Most rules control actions for specific conditions. When an event is described, specific actions are prescribed because of it, for example,

A gross margin rule: If a product ROI is below 18 percent, discontinue sales of the product.

A payroll rule: If an employee is late for work five times in a month, dock one day's pay.

A purchasing rule: If a vendor fails to deliver on time three times in a year, secure another source.

Thousands of business rules (documented or word of mouth) exist in even a small business. Formulas for reordering inventory can be highly complex rules frequently executed by a computer. Company policies and procedures are business rules. Most organizations could not operate without rules, just as countries cannot operate without laws.

Management must consistently review and improve business rules.

How good are the company rules?
    As good as the people making them?
    As good as the people using them?
    As good as the people enforcing them?

The business rule problem is frequently ignored. Problems are allowed to fester before rules are created. The business system is a set of rules. Rules fail when they

1. Are not precisely defined
2. Are not well indexed and accessible
3. Are overridden frequently
4. Are not enforced
5. Are not communicated
6. Are inconsistent with other rules

Many business managers argue that more productivity is lost by confusion over rules than any other subject. It is a strenuous effort to organize and to perfect the rules of a business. It is even more complex to communicate them downward.

Business rule changes are among the most illusive type of information. Many companies point to voluminous binders that are supposed to describe their business rules. However, the current practice, in most instances, is to update them every five years. Most business rules are obsolete the day after they are initiated and never describe why the rule exists.

One problem is that the rule creators are not the doers. The doers change the rules to what works best for them or whatever seems appropriate, instance by instance, irrespective of the impact on other business units.

With the introduction of the computer into the work force, rule creation and updating have enforced more discipline, but they have also created more apathy toward improving the rules.

Most companies do not have a central index or even a schedule for maintaining and reviewing their rules. Opposing rules may never be found except in instances when they collide. Competing rules can run side by side, costing companies a fortune.

The knowledge about the rule relationships can and should be addressed as a major company effort using regular reviews.

Continuous rule evaluation is a subject for every manager. Most managers are conformists, not rule analysts. When management has not provided a way for rules to be located, reviewed, related, and updated, rule precision has been severely crippled.

In Chapter 5, we will discuss how business rule specifications can be classified and computerized. Management must ask to inspect the business rule book.

> Management frequently asks how to index, relate, and review its business rules.

BUSINESS INFORMATION INTEGRATION

What is information integration? From the previously discussed business subject classifications, it is clear that they do not stand alone. They need to be related within a consistent overall context. For information to exist, major subject types need to be joined.

When business subjects are joined, they create information linkages. These relationships are called an integration view or a pathway. For example, see Figure 2.3.

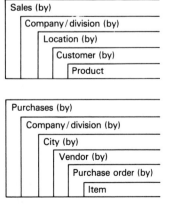

FIGURE 2.3　Business subject integration views (subject binding).

In most businesses, the process of joining business subjects is a hodgepodge of duplicated random views. What is not immediately obvious is that there can be a finite limit to the number of integration views required to describe all business subjects and relationships. This limit to the number of information views simply requires that the information type instances *always* follow a single standard sequence using uniform generic words.

When this naming discipline is not imposed, the cost of business information processing expands to meet the unlimited vocabularies of systems analysts, business operatives, and passersby.

Why Is Knowledge Integration Needed?

While the cost of information duplications is significant, the time required for business operatives to interpret information meaning out of thousands of different inferences, schemas, and contexts is a real profit-killer.

Subsequent chapters in this book discuss in detail how information costs can be controlled using a limited number of integration chains. The reason this idea has not been developed previously is probably due to the lack of a disciplined concentration on knowledge as an asset for reuse.

As business computerization takes place, it can mistakenly focus on islands of separate applications, such as

Sales entry	Receivables
Purchase entry	Payables
Inventory	Payroll
Manufacturing	General ledger

Separate files, separate systems, and partitioned thinking result. Integrated thinking about the whole command and control system is frequently not applied. Without a holistic view of the entire business, it is impossible to optimize the interaction of all of the parts.

Why is the integration of company knowledge and information worth the investment? The reasons hinge on the productivity and decisions of people and on their prompt actions. Information is receding from the traditional fixed historical report and moving toward immediate in-process status inquiry.

Technology has afforded the opportunity to focus on specific questions and discrete answers. Fixed reporting frequently results in the need for yet another report for the next level of detail. If a manager must manually correlate two or more reports, time is lost, and decisions become flawed.

Therefore, information must be constructed in a relational architecture so that nomenclature, sequence, and statistical correlations are rule driven with decisions prompted in a consistent way. If the information and rules are not initially structured in a logical way, technology will only speed up an illogical process.

SUMMARY

Business information consists of a broad range of subject areas. This chapter indicates that knowledge flows from information and that information cannot be logically controlled without first separating it into classes and types.

Only after classification is information ready to be related and integrated.

The classifications discussed in this chapter are only a partial example of how a business may want to classify its knowledge and information. Detailed instances of the classes are displayed throughout this book. Each class has several related subjects, and the subjects may be hierarchical within their class.

The context of a company knowledge base must embrace all of the information chains that relate to the major measurements of the business. The formulation of relational chains requires a major project specifically to control the knowledge asset. A business must create a *chart of information* similar to a *chart of accounts* that can display the impact of all business activity related to the profits of the global business, rather than merely isolated departmental or specific business applications.

A global perspective discards fixed-type reporting and facilitates a question-and-answer query environment. The result is a prompt to link business subjects with meaningful actions.

A query environment demands an architecture that represents a human recallable schema for easy access to any information of the company information base.

Business operatives, administrative staffs, computer technicians, and the computer itself must have an identical view of the total knowledge base contents. Information fails if it is not organized within one uniform context, common to all. Chapter 4 describes how business knowledge and its rules can be standardized, expressed, and integrated as a single view.

The purpose of this chapter is

1. To present a broad view of types of information that need to be categorized
2. To emphasize the need to formulate knowledge within a globally oriented business context

Knowledge relationships are a major investment that managers will want to understand before they invest large sums in the next round of computer technologies. Knowledge organization must be a major obsession of strategic planning.

A strategic objective is to create a total business knowledge infrastructure and then to automate it as a tool for business managers to use as a profit generating facility. Figure 2.4 consists of a few of the subjects and relationships involved in creating a function knowledge base. The knowledge inventory is a very disciplined warehouse of dynamic information types. Figure 2.5 is a relational view of a business profit measurement model to which the knowledge base can be related. A business enterprise model is a strategic asset of any size company.

A Strategic Company Objective
Create a global business knowledge infrastructure that relates company information to its business rules.

FIGURE 2.4   Business knowledge infrastructure, a change to a global perspective.

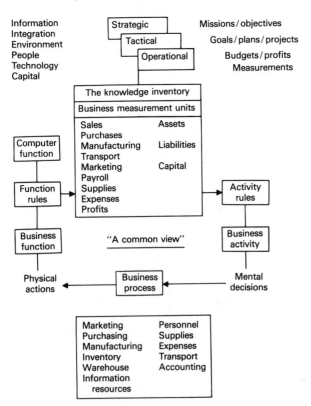

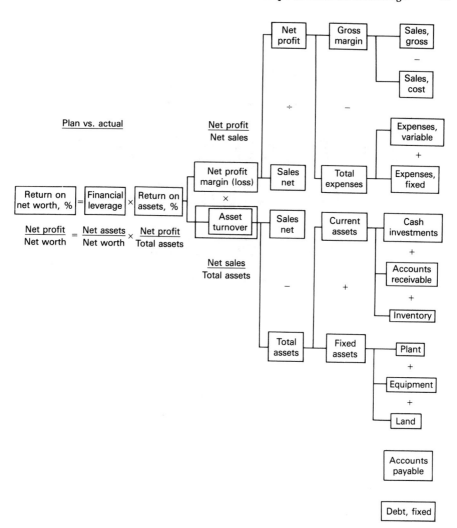

FIGURE 2.5   Business profit measurement model.

Chapter 3

The Responsibility for Business Knowledge

INTRODUCTION

Knowledge—its creation, organization, and distribution—begins as an activity of management. Information must be integrated with business processes. When information is not constructed to relate consistently from strategic to tactical to operational levels of detail, business processes cannot be expected to work optimally together.

It is this author's experience that managers spend more time trying to analyze information contents and results than ensuring that those who can produce results obtain the information they need to act.

If management asumes responsibility for a higher quality of information, the cost of that information can be substantially reduced by the elimination of volume.

Traditionally, technological and information changes affecting professional, technical, administrative, and office jobs come about slowly. In recent years, the tempo of change has been increasingly driven by more and more technological tools looking for a home. Too much technology too soon has resulted in unforeseen costs, breakdowns, and needless complexities. The process of changes imposing changes, before the initial change is understood or stabilized, has forced management into a knowledge gap.

The pressure to increase productivity and performance with new technologies and with the *upskilling* and *deskilling* of employees has resulted in labor cost shifts to technology, work force reductions, and the removal of decision capability from those most able to prescribe solutions.

Unfortunately, some kinds of information pursue trivial subject details such as counting the trips to the lunchroom or keystrokes per minute. Excess information selected by people for others has denigrated skills and eliminated knowledge expertise about the total context of what is going on in the "very big corporation."

The information and technological revolution is slowing because it is out of control, not because technology is bad. The total organization is now involved, not simply a few pieces.

Many managers elect to do the popular thing rather than to make the hard choices that the real knowledge revolution demands. In many companies, culture, politics, passion, and imperfection supplant the discipline, reason, and torture of thought required to enhance and automate knowledge.

Some managers in business really do believe in a disciplined approach to information. Many others are unconcerned about the cost of the data blizzard. Without conservative leaders, imperious to parochial demands, staffs will continue to revel in the prestige of the latest technology. They will continue to participate in many piecemeal technological scams under the guise of departmental efficiency.

Many vendors of information software and hardware release version after version of products, leaving the cleanup of bugs and the retraining of people to their client companies. In-house technical talent is wasted trying to understand and perfect one technology upgrade after another.

Corporate executives must first orchestrate the construction of the new computerized knowledge base. Only then can business managers demand that vendors of hardware and software furnish products to support it. Management must act when the business knowledge is not modularized to readily accept changes.

Knowledge chaos exists
- In most U.S. businesses
- In spite of high investments
- In functional automation

INFORMATION RESPONSIBILITY

Organizational Failures

Historically, the content of information below the level of financial statements has been isolated in separate departments.

In many instances, the requests for information have had to wind through a series of competing priorities and projects within a central computer department. Today, however, it is not unusual for each business department to acquire its own microcomputers, programmers, packages, or outside consultants and proceed to manage its own data processing activities with the full blessing of senior management.

The life cycle of system changes within the centralized data processing organization failed because change took too long to meet the needs of individual departments. The result was usually a static information dinosaur. The systems of information took too long to modify, update, or add in a controlled way. Every change took time to first dismantle what previously existed before the new requirement was produced.

The reason for the problem was that the systems were not constructed modularly to accommodate change. Management did not understand knowledge construction techniques and truly believed a solution was to give every employee artist a personal computer. This solution was soon discovered to yield many more smaller but nevertheless static dinosaurs.

The fact that microcomputers have a relatively low cost enabled each department to acquire and accumulate its own data bases. The cost of departmental staff to utilize the new machines seemed infinitesimal when only a few isolated applications were introduced. However, the need to join interrelated rules and information was soon exposed. This was followed by a need for complex networks to draw it all together again, which was exactly where the initial centralized problem began. The cycle of organizational independence of information failed in a barrage of computer technology changes.

Local area networks (LANs) purport to connect many business operatives to common computer files at one site. Other networks link remote physical sites. Network technology has set off round after round of hardware types and connections, under the guise of increased efficiency, without addressing the core of the problem, information dichotomy.

In this piecemeal approach, managers may once again remain aloof as the duplication and redundancy infiltrate the total organization. The cost of data handling can be disguised within individual departmental budgets. The isolation of departmental knowledge continues to be tolerated.

Managers know the higher costs of dissimilar hardware, programming languages, software packages, versions of operating system software, people training, and information translation variances. Ironically, these obvious diversities are virtually ignored. Information planning and structuring has once again not taken precedence over the technological automation of tasks.

Almost every human task is supported or in some way influenced by computerized automation. However, a piecemeal mechanization has rapidly become counterproductive. The functional people cost savings is not offsetting the lack of knowledge and skill upgrading. The long sought after lower labor cost is becoming incrementally more difficult to achieve.

Why are technological upgrades primarily focused on how computers work rather than on how businesses make profits? Aggressive managers can no longer ignore the excesses of disjointed information. The price of the computer is dropping, but the number of applications, change requirements, and technical staff wages are skyrocketing without adding to the bottom line. More types of word processing, spreadsheets, data bases, and graphic technologies, without knowledge architecture, only erode profits and lose the strategic advantage. Organizational units must ultimately accept global information standards to achieve effective interaction.

The lack of organization knowledge integration can be compared to *separately* engineering automobile engines, frames, tires, and transmissions and then expecting all of the assemblies to work effectively together. Management must recognize the value of a global information construction discipline.

> When a business allows all business managers to avoid information standards, computerized tools are less effective.

Knowledge Fragmentation

Yet another aspect of the lack of information integration is the partitioning of human labor. Too many managers are immersed in microcomputer trivial pursuit. Many have forgotten why they were hired. They have lost profit and productivity incentive. Major opportunities exist in the merger of information and the combination of business activities, not in their fragmentation.

Managers cannot take their jobs seriously when they have become robots with little or no participation except to check up on the computer. They actually become psychologically disruptive when their self-perception is that the computer has taken away their "knowledge" and ability to effect change.

The lack of access to information definition and to the number of translation steps needed to understand and change computer functions has been one of the most neglected phases of recent technological substitution.

Conversely, the emphasis on participative interaction with computerized rules could optimize productivity and exact personal fulfillment. Fourth-generation computer languages have been touted as a solution to multiple file access. However, computer languages are only tools and cannot substitute for the organized business logic to utilize them. Knowledge organization can reduce the number of business management levels required.

> Middle management costs increase if people layers
> only function as translators and relays.

A target must clearly be to capture the knowledge of middle management. The paradox is that those who could support real progress in knowledge consolidation will not upset the power organization equilibrium or eliminate their own jobs. They will thrive by maintaining the information fragmentation and complexity that exist. They will keep the wheel (computer) replacement game going at any cost. A change of perception and incentive is needed to break this gridlock.

Paternal companies that take pride in providing a safe haven for mediocre managers will have to do an about-face to survive. This will probably only happen when their competition establishes a workable knowledge structure.

Some very aggressive companies are already addressing the information engineering potential. Frequently, however, they have become obsessed with massive and costly studies into which the entire management is drawn to the point of exhaustion. High-level business system planning studies are undertaken time after time, only to fall by the wayside. Why?

Many efforts fail because the missing knowledge and information architectures, which could establish a permanent knowledge platform, are missing. Knee-jerk mentality is often directed to panacea software packages, hardware, data communication, office automation, or a facilities contract as quick technical fixes. Some of these actions are clearly abdications of the will to create and manage the knowledge resource.

KNOWLEDGE MANAGEMENT

When knowledge is described as an asset of a company, it is usually referenced in terms that are vague and intangible. No one takes responsibility for it, yet everyone is responsible for it. Many companies talk about this subject, but only a few do much about it.

A purpose of this book is to describe the components of the knowledge investment and to show why and how it can be organized to increase profits.

Knowledge management is a term that implies that all information produced for and collected by or about a company needs to be identified, organized, and managed. Knowledge is an asset of the company. The knowledge base directs and controls people toward productive work. The value of this asset is potentially much more than what it costs to acquire.

Before information about knowledge can be evaluated or managed, it must be organized, standardized, and related so that it can be used effectively.

Knowledge management involves much more than keeping an alphabetical dictionary, a list of reports, drawings, or blueprints. The knowledge facility requires the organization of all of the information for and about a company: a very large effort.

A bill of material (of information) is required to describe all pieces of the knowledge inventory. A bookkeeping schema of how it is controlled is also required. The knowledge system is a business process within itself.

In the previous chapter a distinction is made among

1. The content of knowledge
2. The names used to index knowledge
3. The technique used to control knowledge

Because the number of business terms and their meanings are so extensive, a computerized tool is necessary to keep track of the relationships of all business entities. A few commercial software packages have been developed that maintain business nomenclature, its description, and the relationships required to track entities. Most of these packages are only in their initial stages of development.

Unfortunately, many of these tools utilize techniques that can require more high-priced consulting contracts and create still more abstract islands of technical software.

Frequently, the project to control and document knowledge requires the deployment of techniques without immediate results. Costs savings are not guaranteed or distinctly measurable with many available packages and methods.

As the importance of business knowledge architecture takes hold, better tools can be expected to be created. Implementing the knowledge project without computerized tools would be impossible.

Companies that would not question the necessity of an accounting system to control financial records, or an inventory system to control products, or a legal system to access laws, frequently have trouble understanding the need to create a knowledge resource system to access and control business knowledge.

The management information system (MIS) refers to a facility where information is computerized and stored. The executive information system (EIS) refers to the facility where all information types can be indexed, related, and immediately accessed.

A purpose of this book is to expose the scope of knowledge management and to provide management with an understanding of what EISs are and how they need to be controlled. Without management understanding and initiation, the knowledge asset cannot be structured.

The creation of a knowledge program is a major investment of staff and money. It can create a major change in business discipline and perspective. Depending on the corporate culture, the time for implementation may be right now, or the culture may never be right.

A companywide training effort is required for this activity. Where individual operatives are used to having it "their own way," great resistance is encountered. For example, the documentation, definition, and exposure of the business rules will have a very enlightening effect on the entire company.

Traditional data processing staffs may not be able to comprehend why business rule definitions need to be exposed. If operational management is tough minded and discipline is high, knowledge programs work. When management has a laissez-faire attitude, it will not work well, because tough decisions will not be hammered out. Old buddy lunches are easier. Muddle-on-through fixes are more popular.

There is consensus among companies that are implementing knowledge programs that they are achieving long-range competitive advantages and cost reductions.

Some of the reasons for this consensus are the following:

1. The cost of information handling and communications is dramatically increasing.
2. Confusion exists with the multiplicity and frequency of technological changes.
3. Information systems developed in a fragmented manner have proven too costly to maintain/change and produce far too little managerial information.
4. The integration of business planning and information processing must take place. Data processing departments have shown they are unable to address this problem.
5. The extended misuse of microcomputers is further complicating and fragmenting information.
6. The total business knowledge is not being accumulated. A staff "departmental specialist" environment is replacing broad relational experience.
7. People tend not to work together without a common information schema. A structure is needed to measure synergy, capture knowledge, and prevent the squandering of computer development resources.
8. A large ROI is expected from a reduction of setup time.

WHO MUST ACT?

It should be obvious that the company information responsibility cannot reside in the data processing pyramid. This business unit has more than enough to do keeping data balanced, hardware operational, and paychecks out on time.

More than likely the data processing leader has achieved this important position through years of technical work. More than likely he or she has never worked in any business area where success depended on selling a product or turning a profit for the company. With only a technical type of background, the perception, instincts, and insights to the changing needs of the business and its products, customers, and services are limited and very difficult to acquire.

Yet, this is the very position to which many managements delegate the very sensitive knowledge issue. The knowledge of *how to* can easily overshadow the *what to* under the guise of technical feasibility. Technical limitations can exist, but mostly the issues of management by information require more political and managerial sense than technical prowess.

Department heads are as frequently immersed in their areas of specialization as are those in data processing. Since information crosses all business organization units, only those who have held many horizontal positions in the company have acquired the grasp and balance of a totally integrated information picture. Financial executives frequently acquire a broad range of business information knowledge; however, without line responsibility in a profit center directly related to products, customers, and vendors, keeping the books is not related to the knowledge of which business rules work under specific conditions.

Frequently, no single department head has the responsibility or authority to position the company for a total knowledge project. Company respect, overall comprehensive knowledge, and experience are vitally needed. Concern for the overall information needs of the total company is an absolute requirement.

By the process of elimination, the knowledge opportunity falls squarely on senior managements. Is any Chief Executive Officer (CEO) fully discharging his or her responsibility when information planning is neglected? While business knowledge is a responsibility of all managers, its chief provider is the CEO. The CEO is the prime communicator. Everyone in the company moves in the CEO's image. The communication of the missions, objectives, and goals must be created and distributed at the right time and place.

Why has the information problem not been previously recognized? The answer clearly is that is has, many times over. Why has it not been solved? Many attempts have been made to create computerized systems for many separate applications of the company. Many managers have sponsored project after project, application by application, package by package, hardware after hardware; however, the adjoining problems only increased.

The chief executive may not

1. Understand the need for a global knowledge base
2. Participate in enough detail to understand the global knowledge base effect
3. Insist on a total companywide information resource management project
4. Link business knowledge support to today's technology

TEN ACTION STEPS

When the CEO understands the knowledge dilemma and decides to initiate action, a strategic decision has been made. If the decision for a knowledge program is not sponsored at the CEO level, the project will not succeed. No one else in the organization has sufficient influence to make it happen.

All operational managers must push the knowledge project upward to the CEO and then allow it to be the CEO's idea. The most effective sponsor may be appointed the project executive.

A knowledge program is difficult to sponsor because the asset

1. Is partially an intangible
2. Is a long-range investment
3. Requires major funding with no immediate payback
4. Affects a total company discipline
5. Encounters political power changes
6. Affects managerial techniques
7. Competes with short-term projects
8. Requires high-level quality planning
9. Is not a new piece of hardware
10. Is an investment in group productivity

When the program is initiated, several broad steps are necessary to ensure success. These milestones are described below. The CEO will not personally be involved in all of the activities of the program. However, the CEO must clarify the results that are expected and that will be personally reviewed. This review type of involvement is the necessary ingredient to ensure a high quality of effort and output. A description of the major activities is appropriate.

1. Establish Objectives

A composite of the knowledge management (KM) objectives is given in Box 3.1. The objectives are what most information engineers believe to be the basis for pursuing the knowlege program. The CEO must create a set of objectives that fit the company performance needs. The objectives describe the change and establish the measurements for the project.

2. Establish the Knowledge-Based Organization

The project executive must carefully select the managment team that will carry out the specific tasks of the program. The team members' broad business knowledge and experience will be as important as their ability to work together in ensuring the quality of the detail work tasks. The project executive has the responsibility to ensure that the program funding is in place and that the right tools are employed to facilitate the work.

BOX 3.1

Knowledge Management Program Objectives

1. Establish a common view of the ideal business: Result = consensus.
2. Define and standardize company terminology: Result = consensus.
3. Reduce the complexity of information and system relationship: Result = productivity.
4. Separate *what* is required from *how* to create it: Result = creativity.
5. Control business decision rules and changes: Result = performance.
6. Provide a permanent planning tool: Result = control.
7. Reduce development and operational costs: Result = resource utilization.
8. Modularize information and knowledge: Result = flexibility.

---

3. Set Up the Information Index and Dictionary Project

As knowledge and its information are formulated, the information dictionary will become the basis of company vocabulary. The team must be prepared to personally adopt the terminology created in the program to demonstrate the importance of using the correct words and meanings for all company subjects.

4. Initiate the Information Integration Project

A major task of the program involves constructing the relationships of subjects that are the critical success factors of the company. The project executive will have to engage managers to ensure that the correct extent of integrated information is identified for every department and at every level of management for all business reporting and transactions.

5. Establish the Business Model Project

A major task of the program involves a definition of all of the business processes, functions, and activity costs of the company and the relational charting of their detail. Since this effort is a permanent documentation of work relationships, a responsibility must be assigned to update changes as a normal part of the business.

6. Establish the Business Rule Project

The identification and indexing of all company business rules are the most time-consuming processes of all of the project work. The tendency will be to become reactive to immediate problem solutions, rather than first documenting what actually exists. The project executive must make it clear that initial reactions should be avoided until all of the business rules can be compared relative to their total effect. The business rules can affect many of the processes identified in the enterprise model.

7. Establish the Prime Business Measurements

The business measurement identification task requires the knowledge of many business experts. It is a long and tedious task to identify which functions of the business require which measurements. The units of measure, time periods, and frequency of occurrences of information for all business functions can have a profound effect on the cost of production. Productivity, performance, and resource utilization are the prime issues.

8. Create the Knowledge Control Center

The knowledge control center is an organization. Its activity at the outset is to index and collect contents of all of the information and rules identified by the knowledge project. This organization monitors all information requests, checks duplications, and identifies who requires what information. This organization will expose what is not reported, what should be reported, and to whom.

9. Provide for the Migration Plan

This task is a plan to change what currently exists. It is a step-by-step series of subprojects to create, delete, and change information and business knowledge rules. This task takes priority over the planned implementation of new technologies.

10. Invoke a Companywide Training Project

This activity is ongoing. It begins as each team has completed a segment of work suitable for presentation to the company business units. The effort engages many of the business managers of the company. Open communication along the way helps to avoid shock by projecting what will be forthcoming. The influence of company internal training will set the tempo for progress and efficiency. Continuous audits are an integral part of this phase of activity.

The preceding are the ten major areas that the CEO must ensure are addressed by the knowledge program. Many of these activities have been attempted by companies as separate projects. It is only when they are approached together in the context of the global enterprise that symbiotic benefits can be achieved. The knowledge program may be compared to what is commonly called a system development life cycle; however, the project is global and will likely be of longer duration because it affects the entire enterprise. Its activities interlock. Box 3.2 is a summary of the ten phases of the global business knowledge program to organize existing work, rules, and information.

BOX 3.2

Knowledge Program Phase Summary

1. Information resource program objectives
2. Information resource program organization
3. Information dictionary
4. Information integration
5. Enterprise model
6. Business rules
7. Business measurements
8. Knowledge control center
9. Migration plan
10. Training and postaudit

SUMMARY

Part One has identified and described many attributes of business knowledge and its information. The emphasis has been directed toward understanding

1. What knowledge is
2. What knowledge is needed
3. Why knowledge is an asset
4. Why knowledge requires management support

A further implication has been that while companies pay lip service to the need to organize and control information, only a few have launched the much needed knowledge program.

Those companies that initiate only isolated systems projects have frequently attacked a management problem with piecemeal technical solutions. Little or no attention has been given to the global knowledge architecture or to the methods by which information and rules are joined to facilitate profits.

Because of poor project techniques and tools, many of the attempts to organize information, business/computer functions, and business rules have failed.

Last, the issue of responsibility was addressed. Whoever takes the responsibility for a knowledge project can dramatically affect the company future. When the CEO is not involved, there is general agreement that everyone loses.

The *what* and *why* of the knowledge management project have been presented from many views. Could they be covered in fewer words? For the size of the proposed project investment, there will probably be even more conferences among managers required to initiate this worthwhile program.

The remainder of this book expands, with more detail, the premise, technique, and context that have been so elusive to date. Hopefully, what follows can become a mandate from the CEO to the managers of their company to initiate a knowledge resource upgrade project.

The *how to* of what follows is dependent on a consensus of the *what*, *why* and *who* of the previous chapters. It would be ideal if the CEO could pursue the following techniques. Where this is not possible, other leaders will have to plan the detail activities under the CEO's general direction.

Part Two pursues a knowledge archetype that can be used for business knowledge organization, construction, and control. Without some type of architecture, knowledge would be too difficult to organize, define, and relate.

> **Note:** The technique described is called business knowledge architecture (BKA). The BKA technique can be facilitated using a computerized tool designated BKA* (Business Knowledge Advisor). BKA* provides a standard relational repository for storing knowledge about work, rules, and information relationships. BKA* is not an absolute requirement to support BKA techniques; however, computerized support greatly facilitates the creation, storage, updating, and access of information. BKA* uses the Oracle Corporation's RDBMS, SQL, and personal computer hardware; however, any RDBMS could be used for this purpose. The BKA* program is not complex and relies mainly on standard name pattern matching.

Part Three describes the activities and tasks required to *implement* a knowledge program. An implementation of a knowledge program cannot be undertaken without the vision, disciplines, standards, and tools described in Part Two. Pitfalls and problems to be expected are also described. Part Three presents a migration rather than a system replacement. Chapter 8 describes the project head-count requirements and consequently alludes to the cost of the total project.

When managers fail to alert the CEO to the strategic discipline required for the knowledge age, we all lose.

Knowledge and information are unifying forces for corporate strategy, culture, and infrastructure.

PART TWO

BUSINESS KNOWLEDGE INFRASTRUCTURE

In Part One, many information deficiencies were described and attributed to a loss of business profits. The need for a knowledge platform for the entire company was emphasized. Business problems were directly related to unstructured information.

Business growth is directly dependent on those managers who take the necessary steps to structure their company's knowledge. If a knowledge strategy is to be put in place, it will have to be advanced two to three years before its impact can even be observed. It is a long-range investment. Many managers already perceive the importance of building architectured information but have not had adequate time to learn what detail is involved or how they are directly responsible.

A knowledge program is a strategic project within itself, not unlike any other business venture. There are many technologies that claim to be "The Road to the Sun" but actually terminate at "Camp Disappointment." It is very easy to be misled by solutions that merely connect computer hardware and program operating facilities. Application software is indeed available that can rearrange data: word processors, networks, windows, spreadsheets, data bases, operating systems, artificial intelligence, and computer design software. These specific tools are only mechanisms and do not create a permanent business knowledge platform.

Clearly, the use of words can change the perception of reality. Imprecise business expressions can confuse truth and values. The language of business, properly structured, can formulate and preserve a road map of experience. However, the mischief of technical language can and does destroy much group productivity.

Part Two

1. Describes a business knowledge morphology
2. Focuses on key business subjects
3. Displays standard business information views
4. Shows how business knowledge itself can be architected/standardized

The knowledge and information architecture to be presented is common to all business systems. After any company's information content is identified, it can be related using standard relational parameters of the following archetype. The perception of context, semantics, and syntax is required to express business knowledge. Without an overall business information platform, many technological tools are rendered ineffective.

The business knowledge architecture (BKA) is a pragmatic solution for identifying, associating, building, and storing

1. Business subject types and subjects
2. Business terminology types and terms
3. Work types and their instances
4. Rule types and their instances
5. Information types and their instances

The standards to be presented provide a framework for naming components of

1. Decomposition diagrams
2. Entity and data flow diagrams
3. Association and property matrices

Information architecture < Consists of > Business subjects, terminology, and information	
System architecture < Describes > Business work and rules	Network architecture < Describes > Business locations/logistics
Business knowledge architecture (BKA) < Integrates > Business work, rules, and information	

FIGURE 4.0 A Business Knowledge infrastructure. Management needs to understand why a global platform is a primary requirement to implementing a business knowledge program.

Management needs to understand why a global platform is a primary requirement for implementing a business knowledge program.

The strategy for constructing architected information is to identify all of the major subjects of an enterprise, using descriptive names and a standard set of access name abbreviations, and then to consistently assemble them in a standard, integrated, relational, and hierarchical way. If knowledge identification standards and principles are consistently used, there will be fewer problems in planning, relating, measuring, and controlling the expansion of the knowledge base of a company.

The sequence of the chapters in Part Two is established in order to first define information standards and then to show the importance of their use to name and relate business processes and entities:

> Chapter 4 describes a global information morphology, basic business categories, types, and class relationships for standard identification.
>
> Chapter 5 describes a business model for work and rule identification using name and construction standards presented in Chapter 4.
>
> Chapter 6 describes an integrated platform for business entities that relate business work, rules, information, and network domains.
>
> Chapter 7 describes a functional platform for remote-site information and network control.

Business knowledge architecture (BKA) is a facility to
    Plan
    Organize
    Locate
    Control
    Integrate
    Analyze
        Business work
        Business rules
        Business information
It is a practical target, not a scientific standard.

Business knowledge architecture (BKA) consists of
        Information architecture
        System (functional) architecture
        Logistics architecture
and takes precedence over
        Computer hardware
        Data base software
        Computer operating software
        Computer applications software
        Computer network software
        Computer-aided software engineering (Case)

Chapter 4

Information Architecture

INTRODUCTION

For three decades, computer technology has been randomly applied to many isolated business applications. Only recently has technology been introduced that can facilitate the organization and understanding of global business knowledge.

The pieces of business data are normally so voluminous and fragmented that business operatives simply cannot cope with their magnitude without a consistent and architected business context.

Many prestigious organizations have recently begun to promote techniques and technologies to model and define how to implement the large-scale integration of company information. Unfortunately, in the rush to exploit technique, some of these innovators have missed a priority axiom of knowledge transfer.

One of these axioms is addressed in the new science of memetics. Memetic engineering exposes basic building blocks of human knowledge retention and communication. The basic component of memetics is called a meme. Memes (building blocks) are referenced in this book as work, rule, and information units. Meme units succeed when they give the business mind a comprehensive way of ordering otherwise chaotic entities. Properly presented, meme units can stick in the mind for a long period of time, cause rapid and dramatic mental change, and present a common business paradigm to inoculate a business culture against the barrage of nonmeaningful business information.

For many years, philosophers, psychologists, neuroscientists, anthropologists, and linguists have researched how the human mind functions. The arguments of rationalists, Cartesians, Kantians, and empiricists such as Lowe, Berkeley, and Locke have collided over how information gets into and stays in our consciousness.

The pursuit of artificial intelligence has introduced still another round in the attempt to replace minds with machines.

In 1956, George Miller's article "The Magical Number Seven, Plus or Minus Two" described the inability of any individual to associate subjects beyond the level of seven items or tasks. The works of Chomsky and Wittgenstein have convinced most cognitive scientists of the worth of simplified syntactical structures. The way around memory and linguistic limitations is to group sets of items together (for example, a set of numbers, abbreviations, or symbols) and then to treat the assemblage as a unit. The business knowledge architecture (BKA) in this presentation does just that.

The human limit for information processing synthesis has encouraged me to modify the BKA many times before presenting it in this book. It had to be tested on many business operative and data technicians. The ability to perceive identical context by both groups was the ultimate challenge.

Business operatives seemed to learn the concept faster than data technicians. However, when data technicians who were high achievers pursued the concept, they were immediately able to relate business information views to computer storage addresses, thus providing a direct access from humans to mechanized information storage locations using pathway names.

It is beyond the scope of this book to consider the impact of inherited or predispositioned mind sets of individuals. The need is for a uniform "global songbook" for the business choir to use in interpreting information placed in and produced by machines.

The following structures should provide a real challenge for those who would try to escape the discipline and rigor that are invoked. Certain properties of the human mind may indeed determine the way symbolic relational language operates.

The use of symbolics to affect human behavior is stressed in the form of abbreviations but can just as well be replaced by icons where the icons are relational. The concentration is on access word abbreviation strings to connect and describe subjects. The richer the abstract mental models can be constructed and implanted to represent relevant business relationships, the better they can be applied to preserving business knowledge and identifying profitable actions.

BUSINESS INFORMATION CONSTRUCTION

Subjects and Terminology

For many years, companies have created what is commonly called the company data dictionary. Computer software vendors have provided software products to log and describe data elements, definitions, and their properties using computer files. The sequence for this exercise was mainly A to Z. If dictionary users knew the spelling of a word, its description, or its abbreviation, they could locate it alphabetically in a compilation of definitions. Clearly, many unique words have become a part of an industry or of a company's jargon.

Most business dictionary maintenance degenerates because anyone's semantics and syntax seem good enough to be used in practice. The dictionary is usually not a high-priority project. The dictionary is a prime example of group productivity, but it has failed in most companies. Few business operatives are even interested.

The practical use of information embraces many integrated words to yield a unique context and meaning. A business dictionary is only a subset of isolated basic particles, like the finite chemical table of elements. When chemical element symbolics are expressed in structured formulas, almost any compound can be expressed.

Similarly, business subject strings can be created with precision using naming standards. The exhaustive number of business subject combinations can be reduced to a relatively few information units.

When organizing the information of any company, it is clearly necessary to create a subject dictionary of company terminology, names, abbreviation/symbols, and descriptions. However, for those companies that seek to preserve business knowledge, a highly disciplined and financial commitment to subject accuracy, consistency, syntax, completeness, and subject relationships is required. A brief analysis and an example of information architectures can expose the knowledge retention problem.

> A major strategic problem of information is its lack of structure.

Specific criteria must be met in order to create an integrated business information architecture:

1. *Completeness*: All business subjects, events, conditions, assets, and liabilities must be available from a common dictionary. (All aliases default to one name.)
2. *Context*: All expressions must fit into a single overall business context from strategic factors to operational history (the whole enterprise).

3. *Syntax*: All business expressions must follow the same formats and rules for construction.
4. *Semantics*: All business expressions must define word meanings with a uniform naming consistency.
5. *Pragmatics*: All business expressions must be compact and simple enough to be accessed quickly using business English, without a clutter of words (one fact per field).
6. *Accuracy*: Each business expression must yield indisputable visual evidence of one singular business meaning. The element name must require no extraneous descriptions to provide a unique meaning (one field per fact).

When a single methodology can meet the preceding criteria, it can be considered usable. Business knowledge architecture (BKA) is an infrastructure that can be used to describe and relate every business subject in a uniform way. Uniformity permits a complete integration directed toward the major profit determinants of a business.

Business knowledge architecture is a global business subject framework. It is a schema for clustering related business entities within a global business context.

The BKA subject types are the highest level used to organize and sequence major business entities. Six subject types collectively form a holistic repository of major business subjects.

They are as follows:

CONTEXT PRIORITY	BUSINESS SUBJECT TYPES	ABBREVIATIONS
1.	Measurement type	BMT
2.	Organization type	BOL
3.	Location type	BLT
4.	Resource type	BRT
5.	Transaction type	BTT
6.	Product type	BPT

A BKA rule demands that subjects from the preceding types couple only in the priority sequence of their type. This BKA rule prevents building duplicate and redundant two-way name strings.

Seven (BKA) terminology types collectively form a similar reservoir of terms that extend and describe business subjects. Teminology types are ordered to provide consistency in their selection and use. They are as follows:

CONTEXT PRIORITY	BUSINESS TERMINOLOGY TYPES	ABBREVIATIONS
1.	Extension type	EXT
2.	Status control type	SCT
3.	Time period type	TPT
4.	Time frequency type	TFT

CONTEXT PRIORITY	BUSINESS TERMINOLOGY TYPES	ABBREVIATIONS
5.	Command verb type	CVT
6.	Unit of measure type	UMT
7.	Value type	VLT

Note: As the preceding subject and term types are described, it is important to remember that they are used to uniformly derive word strings. The word strings are then used to uniformly create consistent business work, rule, and information access names (a two-step operation).

BKA subject/term combinations provide a global business semantic diagram that facilitates business subject recall by business operatives.

BKA goals are

1. To construct unique/uniform subject names (elements)
2. To construct work, rule, and information combinations using uniform abbreviated subject name strings

The result is a single global integrated array, without the need for further name translations. A global set of related information tables is created where any information combination can be created and retrieved using subject keyword strings.

Subject type/subject/term combinations can be expanded and updated within the business context. They provide a long-term, reusable, and unified framework for related subject tables. The categorical matrix provides a logical organization for business information expansion and control for the entire business enterprise.

Subject/term type combinations provide a context with which to construct, correlate, and control information statements, views, rules, questions, and answers from the highest strategic level to the lowest specific element of knowledge identification.

Note: BKA* is a computerized software support tool that allows subjects and terms and their derived work, rule, and information names to be created, deleted, updated, queried, and cross-referenced. It uses the Oracle Corporation data base and the SQL language. BKA, as a *technique*, does not absolutely require BKA* software. However, the voluminous collections of data found in an enterprise make nonmechanized control of data too cumbersome.

Due to the importance of the subject/term priority concept, each of the types will be described in depth. Both horizontal and vertical usage priorities exist within subject types and between subjects and terms of their respective types. Figure 4.1 displays four levels of major business subjects: types, names, attributes, and references. Figure 4.2 displays four levels of terminology resources: types, names, attributes and references.

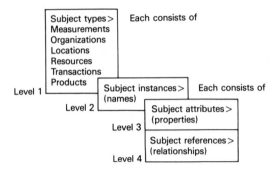

FIGURE 4.1
BKA—business subject levels. Major business subject names are used to identify all business work, rule, and information statement names. Business subjects are organized by type and tabularized in subject type table. Subjects are concantenated to provide relational names reflecting subject associations and their source tables.

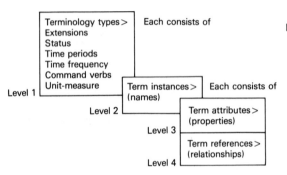

FIGURE 4.2 BKA business terminology levels. Terms append to major business subjects and extend the meaning of subject related permutations. Term abbreviations and acronyms are used in a consistent term type priority.

Business Measurement Type (BMT)

Business measurement units (BMUs) are members of the BMT. BMU's are the major measurements of business events, assets, and liabilities. Values of these subjects are used to measure and calculate the critical success factors of a business, for example,

> The utilization of resources
> The events of the business
> The magnitude/value of business assets/liabilities
> The flow of business funds
> The ownership of the business
> The profits of the business

Business measurement subjects are prioritized according to the way a company presents its financial statements. Each measurement unit is a focal point of analysis for the mainline business processes. The business measurement units are the prime key platform to which all business subjects can be coupled.

Box 4.1 is an example of business measurement units and their abbreviations. Any company may create and define its own measurements, but the content will be similar to that shown in Box 4.1. Business measurements are the equivalent of a business *chart of accounts*.

Note: A finite set of reusable BKA abbreviations/acronyms is used for subject references. BKA abbreviations are three-character sets followed by a one-character delineator.

Traditionally, business measurement *accounting* units are the foundations and prime keys for classifying, indexing, and tabulating business information. They must be selected with care.

BOX 4.1

Business Measurement Units (BMUs)

SLS.Sales
PUR.Purchases
INV.Inventory
MFR.Manufacturing
TRN.Transport
GRM.Gross Margin

MKT.Marketing
PAY.Payroll
ADV.Advertising
SPL.Supplies
EXP.Expenses
INC.Incomes

PBT.Profit before tax
TAX.Taxes
PAT.Profit after tax

CSH.Cash	A/P.Payables
IVT.Investments	DBT.Debts
A/R.Receivables	BND.Bonds
F/F.Furniture/Fixtures	STK.Stock
EQP.Equipment	CAP.Capital
PLT.Plant	
LND.Land	

Business measurements are the critical business knowledge & success factor references.
Business measurement units are a key knowledge index.

Time Period Units (TPUs)

Three time period units (TPU) are qualifying parameters/extensions of the BMU context. Three TPUs establish a time horizon to which BMU information refers. The relational context of strategic, tactical, or operational information is denoted using the TPUs as follows:

1. *Inprocess (INP)*: Implies that events and conditions are underway yet not accomplished, such as sales-in-process (SLS__INP)
2. *Planned (PLN)*: Implies that events and conditions have not commenced yet are expected, such as purchases planned (PUR__PLN)
3. *History (HST)*: Implies that events and conditions have occurred and are completed, such as inventory history (INV__HST)

BKA rules demand that a time period unit must always directly follow a BMU when the full syntax of an information statement is expressed. The inprocess (INP) default exists when either the plan (PLN) or the history (HST) designation is omitted.

Inprocess (INP) is the highest order of precedence because the events may still be affected or altered.

Plan (PLN) is the second order of precedence because adjustments can be made for future events. The lowest order of precedence is history (HST) because historical events cannot be changed even though they may indicate what might be expected to repeat in the future.

The TPU establishes the time horizon for measurement information. BKU time periods are needed to define unique values.

Meaningful measurement (access name) abbreviations are important for the human recall of relationships and for key names in computerized queries.

Business Organization Type (BOT)

The business organization type (BOT) consists of subjects that describe the way a company internally organizes for work and identifies its work domains.

These subjects are fully controlled by and within the company but are not necessarily equated to an organization chart. Figure 4.3 is an example of an internal business organization hierarchy. Clearly, there is a relationship between BOT subjects. Higher-order subjects consist of lower-order subjects in the scope of business work. In addition to the hierarchy between subjects, each organization unit (BOU) can have one or more instances, for example,

ORGANIZATION UNITS (BOUs)	SUBJECT INSTANCES	ABBREVIATION
INC.CORPORATION	INTL-BANC-CORP	INC. = IBC.
DIV.DIVISION	MANUFACTURING DIV.	DIV. = MFR.
PDL.PRODUCT LINE	HEALTH CARE PRODUCTS	PDL. = HCP.
MKT.MARKET	DOMESTIC USA	MKT. = USA.
REG.REGION	WESTERN	REG. = WST.

ORGANIZATION UNITS (BOUs)	SUBJECT INSTANCES	ABBREVIATION
DST.DISTRICT	NORTH ILLINOIS	DST. = NIL.
BRH.BRANCH	CHICAGO	BRH. = CHI.
DEP.DEPARTMENT	SALES	DEP. = SLS.
JCL.JOB CLASS	MANAGER	JCL. = MGR.
PRC.PROCESS	WAREHOUSING	PRC. = WHS.

The naming and relational structuring of the BOU subjects can have an enlightening effect on management. It is one of the major activities in the classification of business work. Each work organization unit must be uniquely named, abbreviated, and defined and related to other organiztion units.

Tables can be constructed for each organization type (BOT). They are populated with that unit's members. BOT tables can be joined to relate the hierarchy of units and to provide binding of related organizational units. (See Figure 4.3.)

Name strings are important where one organizational table must reference or encapsulate another organization table.

FIGURE 4.3 Business organization subjects (unit encapsulation example).

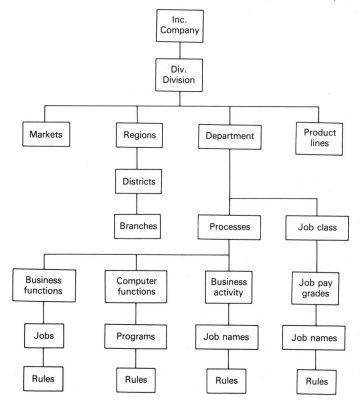

Meaningful organization (access name) abbreviations are important for human recall of relationships and for use as keys in computerized queries.

When business organization relationships change, all of the historical information about them can require modification, consolidation, and archiving. Rules are required for these consolidations, especially for time period comparisons. These relationships are usually maintained as computer file tables. If they are duplicated in several unique computer programs (applications) or multiple tables under different names, their changes can be exhaustive. When no internal company responsibility exists for BOT accuracy, information quality deteriorates.

When the BOT subject type is expressed during the course of the information planning activity, defaults can exist within a type. For example, if a region is referenced, it clearly

1. Defaults upward to its division and its company
2. Projects downward to its districts

In addition to the BOU internal hierarchy, a relationship exists with the measurement unit (BMU) and its appropriate TPU, for example;

```
BMT\TPT\BOT      >SUBJECT TYPE RELATIONSHIPS
                 >SUBJECT INSTANCE RELATIONSHIPS

SLS_INP_PDL      Sales inprocess     (by)    Product line
PUR_PLN_DIV      Purchase plans      (by)    Division
INV_HST_DEP      Inventory history   (by)    Department
```

These relationships can be combined to depict both inter- and intrarelationships of the subject types and subjects, for example;

```
BMT = SLS.    SALES
TPT = INP.    IN-PROCESS
BOT = INC.    (by) Company
BOT = DIV.    (by) Division
BOT = MKT.    (by) Market
BOT = REG.    (by) Region
BOT = DEP.    (by) Department
BOT = PDL.    (by) Product line
```

These relationships can be referred to as views or pathways.

Standard relational symbolics can be utilized to join subjects to form a new subject.

The symbolic "\" indicates subject type to subject type binding.
The symbolic "_" indicates subject instance to instance binding.
The symbolic "=" indicates subject instance to value binding.

The BOTs display an inclusive relationship between each level in their hierarchy. For example, regions consist of districts, and districts consist of branches. Not every company has a BOT directory identical to that shown in Figure 4.3.

In an initial observation, it may not be clear that the business functions or activities belong within the BOT. The structure is for the purpose of subject naming and indexing and not for the purpose of constructing a management responsibility chart. Upon close examination, each BOT unit is in fact a work unit unto itself. Each requires a unique name and can be constructed as a table having its own unit members.

How a business organization maintains its BOT index is a major factor in minimizing its data handling costs. The nomenclature assigned to each BOT subject and instance is a not-so-obvious determinant of how easy its control and retrieval will be. A central control of BOTs and BOT relationships can help to keep the company information meaning from disintegration. Also, management organizations can change frequently. Information needs to be kept updated to support the most current organization structure.

> Information reflects the character of the organization that it supports. It is no better than the management discipline that it facilitates.

Business Location Type (BLT)

The business location type consists of all subject unit names that exclusively describe a physical location of the business organization.

The BLT subjects do not reference noncompany or external-entity locations but only those locations relating to the company itself where internal work takes place.

The BLT subject type vertical relationships begin with the highest level of geographical or geopolitical boundary that describes where a BOU is located. Each successive lower level refers to locations within a location until the smallest definable space has been identified. Figure 4.4 is an example of what needs to be defined and named for each business unit.

Each company must define its own location subject names, hierarchy, and instances in order to relate them in context with their BOU units.

The BLT is the third subject type used for business information integration. The BLT maintains the location level for all subjects within the global work, rule, and information context, for example,

```
BMT\BMU     SLS.Sales (by)
BOT\BOU     DEP.Department (by)
BLT\BLU     CTN.Country
```

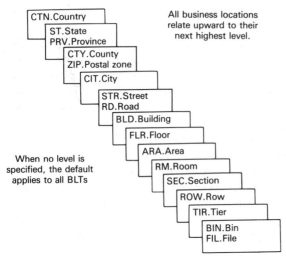

Business location units consist of other business location units.

FIGURE 4.4   Business location types (subject encapsulation).

Some examples of the BMT\TPT\BOT\BLT type strings may help to display how subject type relationships can sequence member unit clusters, views, and substrings:

Sales inprocess (by) Division (by) City
SLS_INP\DIV\CIT
Sales inprocess (by) Market (by) City
SLS_INP\MKT\CIT
Sales history (by) District (by) State
SLS_HST\DST\ST–
Inventory plan (by) City (by) Building
INV_PLAN\CIT\BLD

The sequence of the subject types establishes a consistent contextual sort for a company information base (a kind of semantics diagram directory system).

Note: Standardizing on a single business subject by type priority expression sequence eliminates thousands of optional views/paths that would otherwise clutter the information location spectrum. The number of expressions involving BMU, BOU, and BLU subjects must be controlled. Without type sequence discipline, many business operatives can spend years duplicating and rearranging data using various aliases and synonyms.

When the information of the entire company is standardized with this type of priority structure, duplicate expressions can be eliminated. A very large data handling cost reduction can be achieved. Subjects and priorities can be more easily remembered by users. Like subjects can be more easily compared.

Those familiar with relational data bases can easily visualize how the subject types are tables that contain subject attributes of the subject itself (table columns).

By having a standard sequence for subject types, the memory of business operatives is consistently refreshed in controlling, storing, and relating information. These sequences are especially useful in the naming of tables and table columns for use in structured query languages like SQL.

The subject type/units described so far are related only to the company. The following subject types are *external* resources of the company. They are less controllable. They have a lower priority in the global BKA information chain.

Meaningful location (access name) abbreviations are important for the human recall of relationships and for keys in computerized queries. Locations bridge company internal information to external resource information.

Business Resource Type (BRT)

The information categories described previously are *internal* to the business. They are organized and controlled exclusively by a company and for the company. They are viewed from the inside of the company infrastructure. This distinction is an important BKA axiom when considering external resource types (BRTs).

Internal business subjects interact with external resource entities of the business. External resources cannot be totally controlled by the company. The contextual view of BKA is from the company outward and not from the external entities inward to the company. The BKA outward view (internal to external) is an important concept in

1. Preserving context, conventions, and protocols
2. Avoiding multiple interpretations of open-ended words

Directional naming (source to target) is important in avoiding some of the following references and relationships:

A customer purchase order is easily confused with a customer sales order.
The company purchase order is easily confused with a company sales order.
A vendor purchase order is easily confused with a vendor sales order.

The same confusion is frequently experienced in the use of business terms such as price, cost, invoice, payment, debit, credit, etc. One company's cost is another company's price. A single-direction view from the measurement types (BMTs) to the product types (BPTs) can offset a variety of confusion, for example, subject type path: BMT\BOT\BLT\BRT\BTT\BPT.

The BRT consists of all of the resource units that the company utilizes or with which a company engages in the course of its business activity. Businesses assign their own unique names to these subject types. (See Box 4.2.)

The resource type includes (BRU) subject units that correspond and relate to business measurement subjects, for example,

BMU SUBJECTS	BRU CLASSES	BRU SUBJECTS
SLS.Sales	Distribution	Customers
PUR.Purchasing	Procurement	Vendors
INV.Inventory	Product	Parts
PAY.Payroll	Stakeholder	Employees
KNW.Knowledge	Knowledge	Knowledge units
EQP.Equipment	Facilities	Technology units

The extent to which control can be exercised over resource subjects directly affects company profits. Box 4.2 is an example of resource subjects and table names that when identified and categorized can be reused in the construction of uniform work, rule, and information statements.

BRU subject control is crucial to the success of any business system. This control is a system unto itself and not a part of any single business application. An ad hoc approach to BRU identification, naming, or control creates high-cost business operations.

BOX 4.2

Business Resource Types (BRT)
(Subject classes and types)

*Distribution class
    CST. Customer
    DLR.Dealer
    LIC.Licensee
    OEM.Manufacturer
    GOV.Government
    ITC.Intracompany
    AGT.Agent

*Procurement class	*Knowledge class
CTR.Contractor	DWG.Drawings
VDR.Vendor	SFW.Software
MFR.Manufacturer	PRC.Procedures
SPL.Supplier	STD.Standards
PKG.Packager	RCD.Records
CAR.Carrier	FIL.Files
ISR.Insurer	TBL.Tables
BNK.Banker	PRG.Programs

*Facilities class	*Stakeholder class
TER.Terminals	EMP.Employees
CPU.Computer units	STH.Stockholders
CPY.Copiers	IVS.Investors
TYP.Typewriters	OWN.Owners
TRK.Trucks	AFL.Affiliates
BLD.Buildings	CPT.Competitors
F&F.Furniture/fixtures	REG.Regulators
	CMU.Community

A business can obtain a strategic competitive advantage by integrating its internal and external relationships in a coordinated infrastructure. Box 4.2 is a more complete example of (external) business resource units. Each of the subject types can be expressed as a table of subject extensions.

Frequently, an organizational subject must be joined to a resource subject to express a relationship of two subjects. When the two subjects are bound, they present a uniquely different context, for example,

BMU\BOU\BRU   SUBJECT TYPE STRING RELATIONSHIPS

SLS_DEP_CST	Sales	(by)	Department	(by)	Customer
PAY_REG_EMP	Payroll	(by)	Region	(by)	Employee

Disciplined and consistent sequence in naming is required to facilitate recalling, joining, and relating subjects from their respective stand-alone tables or files. There is a need to uniformly express and control which tables must be joined to access a string of related business subject values.

Many identification numbers (IDNs) are required for resource entities. The syntax for IDN control is worth consideration. A customer may have many IDN.Identification numbers, for example,

	ABBREVIATION
Customer's Dun and Bradstreet number	CST_D&B_IDN
Customer's self-assigned number	CST_IDN
Company-assigned customer number	INC_CST_IDN
Company-assigned customer account IDN	INC_CST_A/C_IDN

A product may have many identification numbers, for example,

	ABBREVIATION
Manufacturer's assigned product number	MFR_PRD_IDN
Company-assigned product number	INC_PRD_IDN
Manufacturer's product substitute number	MFR_PRD_SUB_IDN
Company-assigned product substitute	INC_PRD_SUB_IDN
Competitor's assigned product number	CPT_PRD_IDN

Traditional abbreviations are varied and usually not controlled. Nonuniform names and references such as the following usually prevail:

FOR VENDOR IDENTIFICATION

VNO : VENNO : VDR# :

VNUM: VENNUM: VEND ID:

FOR CUSTOMER IDENTIFICATION

C# : CUSTNO: CNO :

CUST ID: CUSTID : CNUM:

When multiple abbreviations for BRU resources are allowed, the number of permutations can reach into the millions. Conversely, quality BRU resource abbreviations can result in lower information handling costs and more accuracy.

BKA abbreviated strings reduce the clutter of long words and standardize on three-character word abbreviations separated by a "_". Meaningful resource (access name) abbreviations are important for the human recall of relationships and for keys used for computer queries.

Business Transaction Type (BTT)

The business transaction type (BTT) consists of the names assigned to business transactions. Transactions have unique legal and financial significance. A transaction type is a collection of data elements. Transactions are required to communicate the full context of a business event. A transaction cannot stand alone without a reference to its resource entity. It is an extension of

1. Organization subjects (BOTs)
2. Resource subjects (BRTs)

A transaction unit (BTU) joins a BOU or a BLU to a resource unit (BRU).

In any business there are relatively few basic business transaction units, but there are many permutations of transaction extensions. Some basic transactions are as follows:

ABV	TRANSACTION NAME	ABV	TRANSACTION NAME
S/O	Sales orders	I/O	Item orders (supplies)
P/O	Purchase orders	A/O	Advertising orders
T/O	Transport orders	E/V	Expense vouchers
W/O	Work orders	C/A	Capital appropriations
X/O	Transfer orders	J/V	Journal vouchers
J/O	Job orders	IVC	Invoices
R/O	Repair orders	PMT	Payments

A company must identify all of its basic transactions. The basic business transaction units can be extended to as many permutations as are required. A discipline in transaction naming and abbreviations can reduce and restrict duplicate expressions that might otherwise exist.

The BTT is the fifth of six subject types that establish a standard for identifying, naming, sequencing, indexing, and abbreviating views essential for a full business context. A BKA transaction must always be bound to its resource subject in order to be uniquely identified. Some of the more common resource\transaction (BRU\BTU) combinations are as follows:

INC_P/O	Company purchase order	CST_S/O	Customer sales order
CAR_T/O	Carrier transport order	SPL_ I/O	Supplier item order

Meaningful transaction (access name) abbreviations are important for the human recall of relationships and for consistent keys for computerized queries.

Business Product Type (BPT)

Business product types (BPTs) consist of hierarchical classes of business product names. In any business there can be many classes of products and models each of which may have a wide array of variations. Some of these variations are as follows:

PRD	Products	SVC	Services	ITM	Items
MOD	Models	KIT	Kits	WAR	Warranties
ASM	Assemblies	DWG	Drawings	PTS	Parts

An enterprise must identify all of its basic products and services with all of their permutations and with all of their substitutions. Product properties and attributes constitute a large segment of product type identification.

Where product warranties exist, it is necessary to reference a specific product to a specific customer. Frequently product drawings must be referenced to identify part relationships to assemblies and bills of material.

Meaningful product type (access name) abbreviations are important for human recall of relationships and consistent keys for computerized queries.

BUSINESS SUBJECT TYPE PRIORITY

All major (BKA) business subjects belong to one of the following subject types. The priority sequence of the major BKA subject types is worth recapitulation. It is a standard for binding subject units.

Priority Sequence

BMT, 1>: The business measurement type (BMT) is the highest order of precedence because it subjects are used directly to describe the profit results and critical success factors of the business. Measurements are the highest priority to which all information must converge, for example, Sales\.

BOT, 2>: The business organization type (BOT) follows in second place because it consists of organization levels that are responsible for the business measurement values, for example, Sales\Division\Market\.

BLT, 3>: The business location type (BLT) follows the BOT to immediately identify the location of an organization, for example, Sales\Division\City\.

BRT, 4>: The business resources type (BRT) follows the relational BMT\BOT\BLT\ string in order to qualify the person or subject entity that is utilized by the business, for example, Sales\Division\City\Customer.

BTT, 5>: The business transaction type (BTT) follows the BRT and describes the business event that joins or associates the enterprise to its resources, for example, Sales\Division\Customer\Sales order and Purchases\Department\Vendor\Purchase order.

BPT, 6>: The business product type (BPT) includes all base subjects that are products/services of the business. All of the preceding subject types provide background context for the company products, for example, Sales\Division\Customer\Product and Inventory\Location\Product.

The subject types and their priority provide uniform components from which to select names, construct priority sequences, and associate major business subjects. The BKA global technique groups like business subjects and provides a consistent way to relationally join tables, tie words to strings, and preserve a global business context between related subjects.

The author does not suggest that the foregoing subject types are the only way of categorizing major business subjects. The priority of subjects may very well be changed by the nature of the enterprise. The emphasis is rather on the need to broadly classify subjects in order to establish a consistency for subject naming and to create intelligible table access keys.

BUSINESS TERMINOLOGY TYPES

The following terminology types consist of resource terms that extend the meanings of the major business subject units.

Extension Control Type (EXT)

The extension control type (EXT) includes word units that are *nouns* that supplement the meaning of major business subjects. Each company must identify commonly used attributive words that extend the more specific meanings of major subjects. When the standard extension units are used, they can immediately append to previously described BMU\BOU\BLU\BRU\BPU subject units. BKA extension terms cannot stand alone or be used as prime subjects. They always require the context of a major subject.

The extension words are indexed *alphabetically* by term abbreviation for ease of access. The number of potential extensions may seem exhaustive; however, finite limitations are imposed by ensuring that no aliases or synonyms exist in the extension repository of reserved words. By carefully controlling the extension index, information handling and display costs are minimized.

An example of subject\term extension unit combinations is displayed in Box 4.3. Many extension (EXT) terms are used in everyday

BOX 4.3

Subjects and Extension Unit Combinations (Example)

BMT\EXT: Measurement units with extension units

SLS_A/C.Sales account   PUR_SCD.Purchase schedule
INV_BOK.Inventory book   EXP_LED.Expense Ledger
PAY_AMT.Payroll amount   CSH_RSV.Cash reserve
A/R_DCT.Receivable discount   A/P_$CR.Payables credit

BOT\EXT: Organization units with extension units

INC_ADR.Company address
DIV_NAM.Division name
PDL_CLS.Product line class
JCL_LVL.Job class level

BRT\EXT: Resource units with extension units

AGT_COM.Agent commission
CST_NAM.Customer name
VDR_DCT.Vendor discount
CAR_MOD.Carrier mode
PRD_SIZ.Product size

BTT\EXT: Transaction units with extension units

CST_S/O_ADR.Customer sales order address
VDR_P/O_TRM.Vendor purchase order terms
DEP_W/O_IDN.Department work order number

BPT\EXT: Product units with extension units

PRD_IDN.Product identification number
MOD_IDN.Model identification number
ASM_IDN.Assembly identification number
KIT_IDN.Kit identification number
ITM_IDN.Item identification number
PTS_IDN.Part identification number

BKA Note: A BTU unit must always be bound to its BRU unit.

---

business terminology. They are easily recognized, interpreted, and used in a variety of extensions. Businesses find EXT abbreviations necessary to identify, limit, and control frequently used objects. As long as there is a consistent and effective use of EXT units, the knowledge context is preserved.

BKA acronyms/abbreviations are used to identify subject/extension unit combinations. Their purpose is to limit the length of statements that might otherwise be a clutter of words. They are easier to recognize and memorize than a nonstandard, inconsistent, random use of terms.

Status Control Type (SCT)

A status control type (SCT) consists of indicators and adjectives that describe a condition or state of a major business subject.

Each company will select its own status words to describe a condition of business events, persons, places, or subjects. Status words can also be abbreviations within multiple word strings.

The status terms describe the condition or disposition of subjects but cannot stand alone without the relational context involving a major subject.

Status members are usually indexed alphabetically by their abbreviation for ease of reference. They are used directly after any major subject that they describe.

While the number of potential status units (BSUs) may appear exhaustive, limitations are imposed by allowing no aliases or synonyms in the status reserved word index. The number of BKA status words is more than adequate to describe the condition of all subjects.

The examples in Box 4.4 show the use of status words with major subjects of different types.

BOX 4.4

Subjects and Status Unit Combinations		
BLT\SCT	LOCATION	STATUS
LOC_CRE	[Location]	[Created]
BLD_NID	[Building]	[Not identified]
ADR_CHG	[Address]	[Changed]
BRT\SCT	RESOURCE	STATUS
CST_ADD	[Customer]	[Added]
VDR_SUS.	[Vendor]	[Suspended]
PRD_DEL.	[Product]	[Deleted]
PTS_DEF	[Part]	[Defective]
ASM_O/H	[Assembly]	[On-hand]

BTT\SCT	TRANSACTION	STATUS
CST_S/O_CCL	[Customer sales order]	[Canceled]
VDR_P/O_ONR	[Vendor purchase order]	[Not received]
CAR_T/O_SPD	[Carrier transport order]	[Shipped]
INC_X/O_DMG	[Company transfer order]	[Damaged]
VDR_IVC_TTL	[Vendor invoice]	[Totaled]
CST_PMT_REC	[Customer payment]	[Received]

BPT\SCT	PRODUCT	STATUS
PRD_DEF	[Product]	[Defective]
ASM_DMG	[Assembly]	[Damaged]
ITM_SUB	[Item]	[Substituted]

Note: When a subject status is identified, the subject being described takes on a current (inprocess) connotation. It can demand the use of a time period unit to reflect *when* the change of status occurred.

Note: A subject status is almost always the result of an action. Therefore, the abbreviations of the command verbs (CVUs) that caused the status change are close to identical to those of the corresponding status units.

Time Period Type (TPT)

Time period units describe specific time frames to which the event or subject belongs.

Clearly the addition of a specific date—day, week, month, or year— can materially affect the context of an information statement. Each company must standardize its own time period units.

Within the time period type (TPT) there are three subtypes that specifically describe when an event occurred:

1. A time period
2. A time period accumulation
3. A time period variance

Many standards can be associated with time periods. Even the sequence of the month, day, year is subject to variances in actual usage. Each company will establish standard time references and their (access name) key abbreviations, for example,

TIME PERIOD UNITS (TPUs)	TIME PERIOD ACCUMULATION
DTE.Date	
YR/.Year	YTD.Year-to-date
QTR.Quarter	QTD.Quarter-to-date
MTH.Month	MTD.Month-to-date
WK/.Week	WTD.Week-to-date
DA/.Day	TDY.Today
HR/.Hour	
MIN.Minute	
SEC.Second	

The preceding time period references are straightforward attributes. They are inserted after any of the extension or status words in an information statement expression. They modify or specify a time period of the major subject's occurrence.

It is frequently necessary to describe time periods in terms of a range or a variance from its time period, for example,

Future month (MTH_FUT)	Using a plus (+) or a minus (−) number
Current month (MTH_INP)	To signify the variance
Previous month (MTH_PRV)	That is, MTH_CUR_+/−_005

Time Frequency Type (TFT)

The time frequency type (TFT) consists of word units that describe the frequency of occurrence of a subject within a time period. A time frequency unit (TFU) is therefore positioned directly after the time period unit (TPU) that it references.

Business information frequently places a value on the number of occurrences of events within a time period:

- Sales occur daily.
- Shipments are scheduled weekly.
- Invoices are produced monthly.
- Inventory is counted yearly.
- Advertisements occur bimonthly.

A company will want to develop consistent abbreviations (access names) for its frequency designations, for example,

TIME FREQUENCY UNITS (TFUs)

YLY. Yearly
SYR. Semiyearly
QLY. Quarterly
MLY. Monthly
WLY. Weekly
DLY. Daily
HLY. Hourly
RDM. Randomly

Frequency units are important when describing business work, rule, and information types.

If the time frequency of business information is too short, the action implied may be too reactive and cause excess work costs.

If the time frequency of business information is too long, the action implied may be too late and cause opportunities to be missed.

Managers must analyze the frequency of information they receive in order to ensure it is consistent with the action that is possible.

Command Verb Type (CVT)

Business command verbs are triggers that prescribe actions to take place in the course of business. Verbs describe actions of the processes, functions, and activities in which business operatives engage. Every business rule requires at least one CVT\unit.

Command verbs are very similar to status terms, previously described. If a verb is executed, then a corresponding subject status will exist. The verb is usually the cause of the status condition of a subject.

The verb (access name) can be easily distinguished from a status word by its *leading* position in a string of subjects or abbreviations, for example,

Action Command Verb
[Cancel]   [Customer sales order]
[CCL]   [CST_S/O]

Status Control Unit
[Customer sales order canceled]
[CST_S/O_CCL]

If the command verb cancels a sales order, then the sales order is in a *canceled* status.

Command verbs are indexed alphabetically by their access name abbreviations for ease of reference. They are used directly before any business subject to display the action they inflict on the subject.

While the number of verbs seems exhaustive, limitations are imposed by allowing no aliases or synonyms in their index. The number of command permutations is more than adequate for any business expression. The global contextual sort is not disturbed by the insertion of a command verb unit within any information view because the key priority subjects maintain the business context.

The following command verb unit (CVU) expressions display their use in identifying both business work and rules:

Subjects and Command Verb Combinations		
TYPE\TYPE	COMMAND VERB	TARGET SUBJECT
CVT\BOT	ORGANIZATION	SUBJECTS
[ORG] [DIV]	[Organize]	[Division]
[PLN] [MKT]	[Plan]	[Market]
[ANA] [PDL]	[Analyze]	[Product line]
CVT\BLT	LOCATION	SUBJECTS
[DES] [LOC]	[Describe]	[Location]
[MOV] [SEC]	[Move]	[Section]
[NAM] [ARA]	[Name]	[Area]

CVT\BRT	RESOURCE	SUBJECTS
[DEL] [CST]	[Delete]	[Customer]
[CRE] [PRD]	[Create]	[Product]
[MFR] [PT/]	[Manufacture]	[Part]
[SHP] [ASM]	[Ship]	[Assembly]
[CNT] [STK]	[Count]	[Stock]
[PAK] [ITM]	[Pack]	[Item]
[TRM] [EMP]	[Terminate]	[Employee]
CVT\BTT	TRANSACTION	SUBJECTS
[CHG] [CST_S/O]	[Change]	[Customer sales order]
[CCL] [VDR_P/O]	[Cancel]	[Vendor purchase order]
[AUD] [MFR_IVC]	[Audit]	[Manufacturer invoice]
[TTL] [EMP_PMT]	[Total]	[Employee payments]
[BAT] [DEP_J/O]	[Batch]	[Department job orders]
CVT\PRT	PRODUCT	SUBJECTS
[ASM] [PRD]	[Assemble]	[Product]
[PAK] [ITM]	[Pack]	[Item]
[SHP] [PT/]	[Ship]	[Part]

It may be clear that the preceding expression strings are used primarily to identify business functions, rules, and indexes related to business work.

Unit of Measure Type (UMT)

The unit of measure type (UMT) is a collection of subjects used to describe all business value classifications. The unit of measure (UOM) references can be classified as follows:

CUR.Currencies	DIS.Distances
QTY.Quantities	TIM.Time
ID\.Identifications	WGT.Weights
CLS.Classifications	DIM.Dimensions
STD.Standards	VOL.Volumes
VAR.Variances	UTS.Units
REL.Relationships	

To add to the complexity, there can be unit-to-unit relationships between UOMs, for example,

UMT COMBINATIONS	UNIT OF MEASURE COMBINATIONS
Distance by time	Miles per hour (MPH)
Weight by dimension	Pounds per square foot (PSF)
Currency by weight	$ Price per ton (PPT)
Currency by distance	$ Cost per mile (CPM)
Quantity by time	Count per day (CPD)

A standard sequence in the use of multiple units of measurement can restrict the number of combinations required. Each business must control the combination of units required to monitor its products and profits.

The accuracy of the units of measure, used in conjunction with business subjects, is crucial to those working with business transactions. The errors and losses resulting from the careless use of the UOM would no doubt retire the national debt. The variance in the number of UOMs used in the business has a direct effect on information handling costs.

The list of units of measure (UOMs) in Box 4.5 is typical of what is required in the business environment.

BOX 4.5

Unit of Measure (UOM) (Examples)

ID\.Identifier type
   CLS.Classification
   REF.Reference
   XRF.Cross reference
   STD.Standard
   VAR.Variance
   REL.Relationship

IDN.Identification number

QTY.Quantity type
   EA/.Each
   TTL.Total
   CNT.Count

CUR.Currency type
   $$$.U.S. dollars
   $PR.Price (sell)
   $CO.Cost (buy)
   $CR.Credit
   $DB.Debit

TIM.Time type
   YRS. Years
   MOS.Months
   WKS.Weeks
   DAS.Days
   HRS.Hours
   MIN.Minutes
   SEC.Seconds

DIM.Dimension
   CYD.Cubic yards
   CFT.Cubic feet
   CIN.Cubic inches
   SYD.Square yards
   SFT.Square feet
   SIN.Square inches
   SMI.Square miles
   RLS.Reels

VOL.Volume type
   BBL.Barrels
   GAL.Gallons
   QRT.Quarts
   PNT.Pints

WGT.Weight type
   TON.Tons
   LBS.Pounds
   OZ\.Ounces

DIS.Distance type
   MI\.Miles
   YD\.Yards
   FT\.Feet
   IN\.Inches

Value Type (VLT)

Value types (VLTs) are formats and characteristics of the value to be expressed for a major subject. There are many designations for value types; however, the business will have to settle on a standard of its own, for example,

Integer
Character
Money
Decimals
Floating point
Date

are all formats that the actual value can assume.

Many special characters can be included in the preceding types to delineate meanings and breaks in formats.

Values may also be combined with mathematical symbols or CVT operators to designate relationships. Some of the symbols are universally accepted, while others depend on the unique computer vendors' choices, for example,

+	Add	#	Number
−	Subtract	=	Equal to
/	Divide	<	Less
|	Either/or	/	Join
%	Percent	×	Multiply
>	Greater	*	All

As a company creates its information statements and knowledge base, its value operators and symbolics will have to be standardized. If businesses utilize vendor software products, variances in symbolics designated by those vendors will have to be accommodated with cross-references to their permutations.

The physical length of values has always been a property of computerized information handling. The number of characters in each element of data is another value control consideration that has caused its own set of problems for a business when expansion needs must be met.

The value type must not be confused with the value content itself. All of the subject categories described exist in order to adequately describe the value content.

Subject Relationships

Subject types establish a priority to connect their respective business subjects. These relationships may be called views, strings, or pathways. They form a directory to allow business operatives a reference to all business information within a single infrastructure.

Subject views have a direct influence on the quality, accuracy, content, and interpretation of information. Views can be constructed to reflect irrefutable visual meanings. They require a disciplined and consistent syntax to be used in conjunction with the use of subject category types.

Generalized expressions are adequate when they relate to a single subject. When the business context expands to multiple subject relationships, general expressions and local jargon flagrantly fail to convey true meaning. People then revert to metaphors, synonyms, euphemisms, aphorisms, proverbs, acronyms, and aliases to connect and relate ideas. The truth is subverted unknowingly, and "you know what I mean" becomes the universal default.

Thousands of human and computer hours are wasted playing games with semantics. The politics of the English language is a subtle and costly business activity. As with the weather, few have the fortitude to forge disciplined shelters that could make interpretation more precise. In the computerized world, the term gigo (garbage in, garbage out) is a cliche for a lack of content. A lack of relational context is a more primary source problem.

For the preceding reasons, subject types and their subjects must invoke consistency and accuracy in information and its construction. Only a few organizations may accept the challenge of information architecture because its high discipline is not perceived to be universally important. Organizations may prefer to fiddle with technologies that permit information to be construed in as many ways as there are people. *Group productivity* is enhanced with a common standard of reusable information architecture. Individual productivity is not so dependent on information architecture, since a person can usually remember his or her personal expressions.

For many years, business management has sought the holy grail of a standard business information infrastructure. The value of this standard lies in the ability to focus on relational meanings. A business information architecture is a *platform* that can use relational data bases, operating systems, networks, and group productivity tools.

The construction of a subject platform is one of the crucial tasks of business knowledge formulation. There are so many business acronyms that the task of building, organizing, and reducing them to a small family of reusable interlocking data pieces would at first seem impossible. Yet, this is precisely what can and must be accomplished. Subject views must describe their own content as well as expose related subjects without the need for extensive dictionary descriptions/references.

Because the extent of words, abbreviations, and acronyms has become so extensive, icons have become very useful in

1. Reducing the clutter of long statements
2. Visually representing related subjects
3. Providing short access names for human recall
4. Providing fast query to computerized tables

The BKA technique relies on standard access names. The business-oriented individual will have little trouble with symbolic strings used extensively in everyday business practice.

Subject abbreviations can be separated and related by the use of connecting metacharacters. Special symbolics and icons are used

1. To display the type of subject
2. To show a linkage/relationship between subjects
3. To describe singularity or instance of each subject

When subjects are placed in a string or a view, their relationships would ordinarily require connector words such as the following:

By	Follows	Replaces
Consists of	Inhibits	Retrieves
Causes	Includes	Seeks
Creates	Involves	Solves
Deletes	Invokes	Supports
Describes	Joins	Uses
Equates	Or	Updates
For	Requires	Relates

In place of these relational verbs, symbolics can be utilized to encode the relationships that can exist between subjects, for example,

(!)	= each	(*)	= all	(|)	= or
(\\)	= related to	(_)	= joined	(-)	= connected
(,)	= and	(=)	= equal to	(>)	= input prompt
({)	= includes	(<)	= output prompt	(#)	= number

When two or more business subjects are placed in a string, they form a new or combined meaning different from those subjects considered separately. A "_" binds subjects and terms in a string. A "\\" binds subject types. For example, note the following:

ABBREVIATIONS	RELATIONSHIPS
BMT\TPT\BOT	Type relationship
SLS_INP_INC	Sales inprocess (by) company
BOT\EXT\BRT	Type relationship
DIV_IDN_VDR	Division (by) vendor
BRT\BTT	Type relationship
VDR_P/O	Vendor (by) purchase order
BOT\BLT\BRT	Type relationship
DEP_CIT_CAR	Department (by) city (by) carrier

ABBREVIATIONS	RELATIONSHIPS
BOT\BRT	Type relationship
PDL_CST	Product line (by) customer
BOT\BRT	Type relationship
INC_SPL	Company (by) supplier

Subject views can involve any number of subjects but do not require a subject selection from every subject type. Several subjects may be selected from a single subject type. The omission of a subject from a view may simply imply that interim relationships are null or are a default to all types. Any subject expression must always remain in subject type\subject sequence.

Whenever two subjects relate, the preceding subject provides the background, context, or *frame* for each succeeding subject. A contextual framework is established as each subject is invoked in the view. The last major subject in any view is the base subject on which all preceding frames focus.

The last subject in any view is extended only by its attributive terms. Each preceding subject in a view may be thought of as *qualifying* each succeeding subject.

The point to be made is that business subjects need to be categorized by both their types and the instances of their type so that like kinds of instances can be remembered by users and easily retrieved using access names. Abbreviated access names can be directly converted into their unique computer storage location addresses. See Figure 4.5.

FIGURE 4.5 BKA business subject type encapsulation.

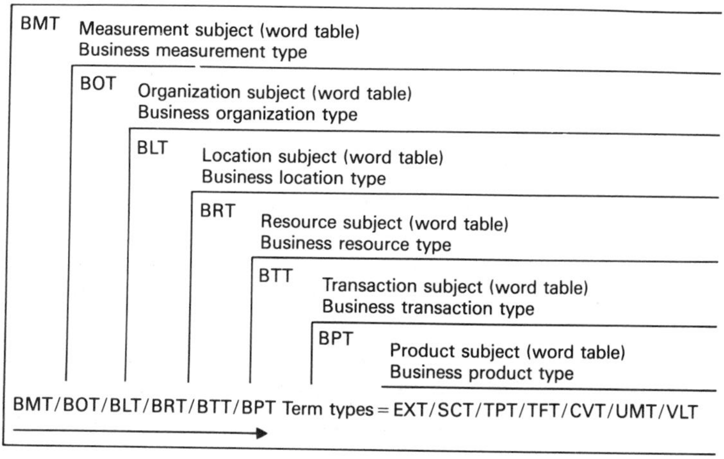

```
BMT  Measurement subject (word table)
     Business measurement type
   BOT  Organization subject (word table)
        Business organization type
      BLT  Location subject (word table)
           Business location type
         BRT  Resource subject (word table)
              Business resource type
            BTT  Transaction subject (word table)
                 Business transaction type
               BPT  Product subject (word table)
                    Business product type
BMT/BOT/BLT/BRT/BTT/BPT Term types = EXT/SCT/TPT/TFT/CVT/UMT/VLT
```

The following are examples of subject-by-subject relationships selected from the categories in Figure 4.5:

INV_DIV_CIT   Inventory by divisions by city
DLR_S/O   By dealer by sales order
PRD_IDN   By product ID number

The preceding subject word strings are constructed by selecting and joining subjects in the priority of the major business subject types.

All BKA naming for work, rules, and information follows the identical sequence of word selection to preserve semantic integrity.

By constructing a consistent set of business subject views, templates are created that can name and index all business information types: subject (X) by subject (Y) by subject (Z).

In keeping with the foregoing rules, business measurement type sequencing provides a high-level index to identify, store, and retrieve all business information. It is advantageous for a business to discretely define the breakpoint between the subject types and their time period units, for example,

SLS_INP, sales inprocess: Categorizes sales events from the time a customer places an order for a product and the product is received by (or shipped to) the customer

SLS_PLN, sales planned: Categorizes sales events (transactions) that are expected to occur at some future date

SLS_HST, sales history: Categorizes sales events that reflect the time after the customer received the product

A/R_INP, accounts receivable inprocess: Categorizes sales events (transactions) from the time customers receive invoices

A/R_PLN, accounts receivable planned: Categorizes the customer invoices or payments that are expected to occur at a future date

A/R_HST, accounts receivable history: Categorizes customer and payments that have been completed

Definitions must be established for each measurement subject for its time class subject combinations.

Business Subject/Term Combinations

Business subject and term type priorities and combinations are a BKA technique for establishing a relational sequence and hierarchy in order to eliminate thousands of data arrays/views/statements that might otherwise exist. BKA is a visual semantics diagram and sort sequence in the context of a global business environment.

An enterprise embarking on a knowledge resource management project must provide for some type of standard information map and index for all of its major subjects and terms in a direct relationship to the profits of the business.

Skilled information architects will recognize that subject types and subject instances are in fact tables, which contain corresponding columns of normalized subject attributes.

Uniform standard names extended using standard terms can provide permanent, reusable sets of information expressions.

The uniform BKA sequence provides a consistent naming method for all business work, rules, and information components. A further discussion of information construction using subject and term strings follows.

Abbreviated strings can be substituted for full words in name strings to reduce the length of the information statements. Uniform architecture techniques such as BKA can greatly reduce the volume, variety, duplication, search, and handling costs of business information.

BUSINESS INFORMATION TYPES

Information types are needed to identify physical collections of related data.

Information type examples are as follows:

Information Types			
FIL	Files	DSG	Data base segments
TBL	Tables	DBS	Data bases
RPT	Reports	TRS	Transactions
DSP	Displays	ELE	Data elements

Because of their close interaction, information units that belong to the preceding types must be consistently and uniquely named so that their name identifies their meaning and so that their name implies a connection to their major information subject(s). Information names are constructed using the previously described subjects and terms.

If information classification is not rigorously applied to information elements, business group productivity can decline because common names can be mistaken for differing information types.

Information types group information units of like kind. BKA information names must be prefixed by major subject units. When information relationships have the same subject in common, they can be quickly related and accessed. When information units have nonsubject names, they are much more difficult to index.

Information instances of each of the preceding types can have the following properties and attributes:

1. Unique identification number (IDN)
2. Time period

3. Frequency of occurrence
4. Response time
5. Text/definition
6. Author
7. Create/update/end/delete date
8. Level/priority/sequence/rank (IDN)
9. Status
10. Format
11. Value range
12. Minimum/maximum number of values

Figure 4.6 displays the levels of information: types, names, attributes and relationships.

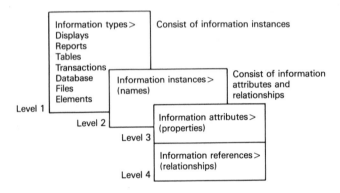

FIGURE 4.6   Business information levels. Information instances belong to physical information types. The names are constructed using the major subjects and terms of (BKA). The uniform use of standard names facilitates subject indexing and query of information. Information units can reference and relate to other information types/units, work types/units, and rule types/units.

BUSINESS INFORMATION UNITS (ACCESS NAMES)

Term extensions append to subjects to form unique combinations called information units (data elements). They refer to unique subjects. One or more subjects are related if they reference the same key data or are column names of the same subject table. Frequently, any information unit can belong to multiple information types, for example,

1. A file can include product element 1.
2. A report can include product element 1.
3. A transaction can include product element 1.

An information unit can be named as follows:

1. Singular (one subject key plus many extension terms)
2. Compound (multiple subject keys plus one or many extension terms)

The naming of a subject element uses BKA subjects and extensions previously identified within subject/term types. Therefore, the first word of a singular information unit is always a major subject name. A subject can be extended by prefixing other subjects to it and by appending term extension suffixes. Some examples of singular information unit combinations are as follows:

ORGANIZATION TYPE

DIV	Division entity
DIV_IDN	Division identification number
DIV_NAM	Division name

LOCATION TYPE

CIT	City entity
CIT_IDN	City identification number
CIT_NAM	City name

RESOURCE TYPE

CST	Customer entity
CST_IDN	Customer identification number
CST_NAM	Customer name

PRODUCT TYPE

PRD	Product entity
PRD_IDN	Product identification number
PRD_NAM	Product name

TRANSACTION TYPE

CST_S/O	Customer sales order entity
CST_S/O_IDN	Customer sales order identification number
CST_S/O_DTE	Customer sales order date
CST_S/O_ADR	Customer sales order address

In each of the preceding examples, the following observations are clear:

1. The subject type is constructed using a BKA subject priority abbreviation as the first word in the string.
2. The term extension can append to any subject (word).
3. The context focuses on a single major subject type.
4. The attributive extension represents a single term, value indicator, or reference.

The ordering of the extension terms is important in minimizing the number of words required to construct a unique view or access name.

Consider the following attributive subject extensions of the sales order subject:

BRT\BTT\EXT	Extension type
CST_S/O_IDN	Customer sales order identification number
BRT\BTT\SCT	Status type
CST_S/O_CCL	Customer sales order canceled
BRT\BTT\TPT	Time period type
CST_S/O_DTE	Customer sales order date
BRT\BTT\TFT	Time frequency type
CST_S/O_MLY	Customer sales order monthly
BRT\BTT\UMT	Unit of measure type
CST_S/O_$PR	Customer sales order $ price

The preceding are singular subject extensions. When multiple subject\type attributes are required, the terminology type can provide the needed consistency.

Consider the BKA sequence of the subject extension that requires more than one extension term:

1. EXT.Extension control units
2. SCT.Status control units
3. TPT.Time period units
4. TFT.Time frequency units
5. CVT.Control verb units
6. UMT. Units of measure
7. VLT.Value units

For example, consider the following:

BRT\BTT\SCT\TPT	Subject type string
CST_S/O_CCL_DTE	Customer sales order cancel date
BRT\BTT\SCT\CVT	Subject type string
CST_S/O_CCL_CNT	Customer sales order cancel count
BRT\BTT\EXT\CVT	Subject type string
CST_S/O_LIN_CNT	Customer sales order line count
BRT\BTT\EXT\EXT\UMT	Subject type string
CST_S/O_LIN_PRD_QTY	Customer sales order line product quantity

In each of the preceding cases it is clear that higher-priority subjects set the framework for and converge to lower-priority subjects and terms.

When *compound subjects* are required to express multiple subject relationships, the Subject Type hierarchy/sequence dictates the precedence of subject selection. For example:

BMT\BRT\TPT\UMT	Subject type string
SLS_CST_YTD_$PR	Sales (by) customer year-to-date (as) $ price

BMT\BRT\SCT\UMT	Subject type string
INV_PRD_O/H_$CO	Inventory (by) product on-hand (as) $ cost
BOT\BLT\EXT	Subject type string
DIV_CIT_NAM	Division city name
BOT\BET\BTT\EXT	Subject type string
DEP_CST_S/O_IDN	Department (by) customer (by) sales order ID-number

Any multisubject extension can be named consistently using the BKA subject\subject\term type priority method.

> **Note:** In relational data tables, the major subject name is the table name. The subject and its term *extensions* are the column names of the table. All BKA subject table column names begin with the table's access name abbreviation. All (BKA) subject relationships within its table begin with the related table's access name.

Plurality

Subject plurality can be expressed using symbolic (icon) conventions. A single element may reference many information types. Members of a subject type may reference a single subject type. A subject type itself must be able to refer to its own *each/all* syntax.

In the subject extension string, the *each* context can be expressed for any subject through the use of the metacharacter "_". When it is necessary to refer to a subject in the *all* context, a metacharacter such as "*" is useful. For example, note the following:

CUSTOMER SALES _ORDER

> CST_S/O_: The background frame refers to a single unique customer. The foreground frame root refers to a single sales order for that unique customer.

CUSTOMER SALES_ORDERS

> CST_S/O*: The background frame refers to a single unique customer. The foreground frame root refers to *all* of the sales orders for each customer.

CUSTOMERS SALES_ORDER

> CST*S/O_: The background frame refers to *all* customers. The foreground frame root refers to *each* sales order within the domain of all customers.

CUSTOMERS SALES_ORDERS

> CST*S/O*: The background frame refers to all customers. The foreground frame root refers to all sales orders for all customers.

It is clear how important this syntax becomes in naming and abbreviating subject element relationships. A simple S/O might otherwise be an unclear expression of its relational meaning. A company must ensure that the *each* and *all* connotation of relationships is expressed correctly.

SUMMARY

Business information has perpetuated its own complexity for too long, simply because it has not been structured, sequenced, or controlled. This lack of information quality has been a major reason for its increased cost and overload on business managers and computer programs. The information may exist, but the effort to identify, interpret, index, redefine, select, and relate it at the time it is needed is exhaustive.

By architecting business information using a BKA type priority context and a standard syntax, the following benefits are achieved:

1. Reduced information costs are achieved when a uniform relational context and names are used by business managers, technical staff, computer programs, and data bases.
2. Reduced information costs are achieved when information is filed/stored in the way it is related in a uniform context.
3. Reduced information costs are achieved when the name of the information accurately and consistently reflects its true meaning. Direct English interrogation is then possible without translations.
4. Faster and more accurate business decisions can be made when human memory is reinforced by consistent syntax and discrete meanings. Group productivity is enhanced.
5. A single relational context for all business information facilitates indexing what exists and exposes what is missing.
6. The use of relational data bases facilitates relational expressions through the use of identical words.

The *how to* organize, name, and relate business data was presented in this chapter as four activities:

1. Create business subject and term types.
2. Create business subject/term access names by subject type.
3. Create business information types.
4. Create business information unit names by type using subject\term combinations.

BKA business information construction requires a few basic rules, most of which were presented in this chapter. Information organization requires a set of standard components, integration rules, and plain hard logical work.

When technical staffs are initially presented with the information architecture task, they frequently have not had the broad business experience or compulsive discipline to rigidly define business subject relationships. Consequently, their names are distorted. In addition, it is difficult for business operatives to see the advantage of uniform information standards, syntax, and semantics as a consistent global context.

Some businesses have operated "on-the-fly" for so long that the human tendency is to "freak out" with the "problem of the day," create more data weeds, perpetuate more confusion, and incur more information handling costs.

Incorporating BKA provides the following:

1. The finite number of subject and term types required to identify all business information is restricted.

2. Unique expressions can be cataloged for reuse by all company departments. The result is improved communication and recall between people and their computer technology.

3. BKA expressions and terminology have a consistency required for a global information infrastructure.

4. The discipline of business information views invokes a higher quality of thought and coordination than an ad hoc assignment of names.

The importance of the principles outlined in this chapter will be apparent in the remainder of this part. The reader may want to review the foregoing terminology, subject\term priorities, and hierarchy within subject types before continuing, because frequent references are subsequently made to them in defining business work and rules.

Rapid advances are being made in computerized software to accommodate thousands of aliases used in the English language. The computerized interpretation of speech recognition and the subtleties of word usage can proliferate rather than restrict the number of dialogs, questions, and answers required to store and retrieve business knowledge. The query-by-example (QBE) translators of (SQL) program parameters still require meaningful and restricted words.

Businesses have a choice to allow any number of systems to expand because the technology seemingly accommodates it. The alternative option is to define and structure a BKA type standard architecture with which all company staff can communicate.

The dilemma of nonstandard nomenclature can be clearly exposed where a programmer refuses to use standard commands of a computer software vendor because of a familiarity with another vendor's commands. The result would be chaos. Artistic individuality of this sort is not permitted.

Yet, the same situation is permitted when a business allows operatives and programmers to avoid information structures because a proliferation of names is accepted by technology.

Uniform information views and access names are keys for the business oriented: (1) question, (2) answer, and (3) command.

The recognition of the need for a technique to relate all business subjects through a uniform information architecture is the first prerequisite for the business knowledge investment.

If information element naming standards are not adopted, the business operative and computer programmer can become engrossed in a complex of secondary translations just to lock in relationships and definitions. The cost of systems change and development is too high and the risk of misinterpretation is too great to continue computerizing garbage, understood only by its creator artist or a single business user.

When businesses purchase diverse application software packages, each with unique vendor nomenclature, commands, and rules, they further proliferate the in-house translation costs for the business operatives and technical staff.

Is that the kind of environment businesses really want to perpetuate when a globally architected knowledge environment is easily within reach?

Many computer hardware and software vendors are scrambling to establish the open systems interconnection (OSI) to provide uniform standards for various computer hardware and networking protocols. After years of proprietary competitive vendor barriers using different protocols, there is a realization that uniformity and standards are more productive for all.

The same principle applies to information architectures and standards within a company and ultimately between companies. Quality products and information are always the least costly.

Figure 4.7 and Table 4.1 show view relationships of information levels previously discussed.

FIGURE 4.7   Information architecture filter.

1. Major business subjects and extension terms are the basic building blocks of the BKA construction tool set.
2. Major business subjects belong to one of six subject types. Terms belong to one of six terminology types.
3. Information views are constructed from subjects and terms. Their types provide a priority sequence for building reusable subject strings and pathways, in a global framework.
4. Information types are categories for clustering related data. They order business events and objects. For example, a report consists of an arrangement of data elements. The report name expresses its relational contents.
5. Information units are word strings that describe a unique business subject and its condition, time period, and unit of measure.

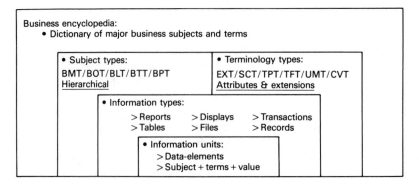

Business encyclopedia:
  • Dictionary of major business subjects and terms

    • Subject types:
    BMT/BOT/BLT/BTT/BPT
    Hierarchical

    • Terminology types:
    EXT/SCT/TPT/TFT/UMT/CVT
    Attributes & extensions

        • Information types:
            > Reports   > Displays   > Transactions
            > Tables   > Files   > Records

            • Information units:
                > Data-elements
                > Subject + terms + value

Table 4.1   BKA Information Architecture (Levels)

Knowledge Levels	Business Information			
	Encyclopedia		*Information Inventory*	
1. Category	Business subject category	Business terminology category	Business information category	The highest level of business knowledge encapsulation
2. Type	Subject types	Term types	Information types	Knowledge types classify like kinds of business entities
3. Unit-name	Subject unit-names	Term unit-names	Information unit-names	Member unit (name) that belongs to its knowledge type
4. Unit attributes	Subject attributes	Term attributes	Information attributes	Extensions of units using their descriptive attributes
5. Unit references	Subject references	Subject references	Subject references	Type\unit to type\unit binding

1. An encyclopedia of subject types\subjects and terminology types\terms provides unique words and abbreviations and sequence, hierarchy, and binding rules in order to standardize business nomenclature.

2. Knowledge levels categorize like types of subjects into lists from which to construct reusable and standard strings of data.

3. By using the major business subject and term combination standards, information of all business types can be constructed, referenced, and associated.

Chapter 5

Business System Architecture

INTRODUCTION

The business work cycle includes all of the activities from a business plan through the deposit of profits in the bank. The business cycle involves all of the business objectives and goals needed to keep the business venture operational and viable. Whether a company is large or small, many of the same functions and activities apply to making a profit. If any one function fails, the chain is broken, and all of the processes strain to compensate for the missing link.

It is important to be able to identify business work, work costs, and work relationships. The speed, smoothness, and flexibility of the business work cycle are a determinant of profits. Before a systematic business analysis is possible, business work must be classified by type and organized as a model so that interactive work relationships and costs can be examined globally.

Business work has many types and levels. Figure 5.1 shows a hierarchy of work. Each work type can consist of lower levels until the lowest level of a work unit can no longer be decomposed or fragmented.

The BKA morpheme defines missions, objectives, and goals as high-level types of work plans. Work is embraced by these high-level statements of intent. Business projects are a work type used to create change of status in work, rules, objects, or information.

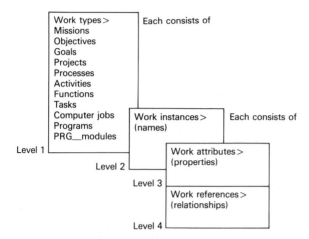

FIGURE 5.1   Business knowledge architecture. Work names belong to major work types. Work names are constructed using the command verbs, subjects, and terms. The uniform use of object (subject) names facilitates the references among work, rules, and information. Work units have their own attributes and properties, for example,

1. Work identification number (IDN)
2. Time period
3. Frequency of occurrence
4. Level/priority/sequence/rank
5. Response time
6. Author
7. Status
8. Create/update/end/delete date
9. Text/description

Each company may create its own corresponding levels of work definition. All work, regardless of its type or level, is expressed and named using a Control Verb Type (CVT) followed by the major business subject/object that it invokes.

Work types provide information engineers with a convenient index of table names for related kinds of work units. To exemplify work decomposition, Figure 5.1 and Figure 5.6 show that both work and rules have the same levels as those previously described for information (types, names, attributes, and references).

Figure 5.2 is a summary of business work types that encapsulate successively lower levels of work types.

BUSINESS PROCESSES

Business processes are high-level clusters of closely related human work functions and activities. When business processes are named and defined, it is better to isolate them from any specific organization, because the

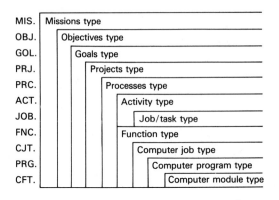

FIGURE 5.2   Business work types (encapsulation). Work object members belong to their work types.

organization may undergo frequent changes. Processes tend to remain more static. Business processes, activities, and functions are logically related. This global relationship is frequently called the *enterprise model*.

The following is a high-level example of business processes:

Business Processes

1. Mainstream
   a. Marketing
   b. Customer support
   c. Manufacturing
   d. Purchasing
   e. Inventory control
   f. Warehousing
   g. Traffic

2. Support
   a. Human resources
   b. Product research
   c. Product engineering
   d. Information resources
   e. Finance and Accounting
   f. Business planning

These business processes are classified as

1. The mainstream processes
2. The support processes

Companies usually assign names to their processes that

1. Describe the work performed
2. Are traditionally familiar to the staff

Business processes can be defined as follows:

A business process is a logical grouping of related work.
A business process can be fragmented into activities and functions.

A business process is not the same as any specific organization or span of authority/responsibility.

How is business system architecture used?

Business systems architecture is used to
- Describe
- Relate
- Analyze
- Sequence
- Control
- Measure
    - Business work
    - Business rule
    - Computer rule
    - Synchronization

Each business process can be fragmented into one or many *functions* and *activities*. The business support processes were typically the first to be computerized in many organizations, probably because their business rules could be more quickly and clearly defined. The accounting department may have been responsible for the computer applications and their development. Administrative cost measurement became the driving force of automation.

Unfortunately, the support processes are not where the most profit-making opportunity exists. When new business strategies, products, or services are to be implemented, the mainstream business processes bear the brunt of success. Information is required to support them.

The total business cycle is the composite of the interaction between the mainstream work processes. Their logical relationships and interaction is the nucleus for high productivity. Unfortunately, many analysts have not explored business process interaction. They continue to implement ad hoc computer software packages for separate "applications" without a complete understanding of the totality of interaction.

As company business strategies and plans are formulated, all of the business processes must be reexamined simultaneously for their joint potential to meet missions, objectives, and goals. Each process can require information of the others. Many processes can be affected by a single rule change. Periodically, company strategies are undertaken and programs are put into action without considering the relational impact on people, processes, or information needs. Of course, this ad hoc approach always misfires, resulting in wasted time and make-up work.

There is always time to repair what is not working as a result of haste but never enough time to plan the job correctly the first time.

The business cycle begins when management starts to plan what the company is going to make, buy, and sell. Regardless of the type of business, some organizational unit will determine what the business is going to do next week, next month, and next year strategically and tactically. All of the business processes in the cycle can require different levels of information for this purpose.

A distinction can be made between the information needed by a process and the information *about* the process itself. The business processes must be organized, and they must contribute information to meet the business objectives.

The processes must be organized to maintain order, eliminate confusion, and smooth the total work flow as business changes take place.

Strangely enough, all business processes, operating at peak efficiency, do not yield the maximum profits for the enterprise. Overcomputerizing in one process while neglecting another actually lowers the efficiency of the total process. Engineers installing a new technique in one process can severely disrupt several other processes.

Traditionally, the mainstream business processes were highly sequential in the way they related (see Figure 5.3). They were perceived as dependent steps. One process typically had to wait for the completion of a preceding process.

> In batch systems a sequential process determined a structure.

Interactive computer technology and its control facility and systems architecture have invalidated sequential delays.

> With interactive systems, the structure determines the process. Consolidated knowledge is its core.

When information is localized to one business process, it may not be integrated in the context of the total business. Information is then not available to describe its impact on related processes. Consequently, people become compartmentalized, and overall business performance stagnates if systems are built solely for each process..

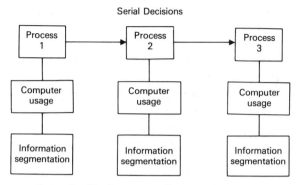

a. Conventional business process fragmentation (sequential)

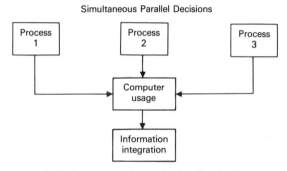

b. Business process integration (synchronized)

FIGURE 5.3   Integrated business decisions.

If computer power fragments information, then the automation to improve only one process materially inhibits the performance of related processes. Unfortunately, this is what usually occurs. Because many processes are automated, sequentially using *interfaces* between processes and information, processes still wait for preceding processes to be completed before the next sequence of work begins.

In a manual environment, "sequential" was the only way people could perform. In a computerized environment, the more automated the process becomes, the less economic the interfaces and delays become. People waiting for work or information comprise a significant business problem. Nonstop systems are the future.

Figure 5.3 depicts the difference between the traditional sequential utilization of computer technology and an integrated simultaneous environment. The information provided for a business application process in the sequential mode is usually measured by one process at one point in time. When the business cycle *pipeline* is increased at only one application point, managers routinely receive their isolated information and make adjustments based on a single unit's information. Ongoing adjustments from other processes simultaneously create a whole new chain of conditions where still more adjustments are required along the process line.

A comprehensive system objective is clearly to provide processing coordination with consistent up-to-date information for all departments. When this occurs, fewer adjustments are required, and better interactive decisions can be made. With this evolution in sight, many companies are racing to integrate their mainstream business processes and to gain a strategic advantage through the use of *integrated* information and business rules.

As an example, computer integrated manufacturing (CIM) seeks to tie the entirety of the total business together: mechanical, electronic, informational, and managerial functions.

Mechanical and electronic integration has proceeded well because the protocols, data rates, and voltage standards are surmountable problems. However, information is a management issue. Its integration has been far more difficult to achieve because information standards and protocols do not exist.

Processes can be classified as analytical or synthetic. In the continuous process, work and its information must move to people. In the intermittent processes, human skills predominate, and people must move to the work. Both classes of work, production and assembly, rely on synchronized information to ensure productivity, quality, reliability, and volume economics.

The integration of people, equipment, and material flow demands the integration and distribution of information about the work performed.

The following is required to achieve work integration:

1. Business knowledge architecture
2. Management will to grapple with integration
3. Resources and expenditures to accomplish integration

The goal is the right information to the right processes at the right time. A champion, the philosophy, and the discipline to manage are needed. No single vendor can put it all together for another company. Integration cannot be accomplished solely by using a type of computer hardware or a software tool.

Using the power of computerized information to prompt business processes can reduce the need for intermediate reports and their middle-management caretakers.

The computer itself can react on a straight-through basis, bypassing middle-management cultural and political conflicts. A few years ago, middle managers scoffed at the idea that computer rules could determine inventory needs or place vendor orders, untouched by human hands.

The withdrawal of cash directly from bank machines without tellers was once a dream. Business rule architecture became a key to automatic decision making in receiving and disbursing cash. These types of automation are only beginning to take hold. Expert and knowledge-based systems are being installed in limited function domains.

When the mainstream business processes are examined, it is clear that they can share common business rules. Their dependencies, however, require information of a much more integrated nature; for example, a decision to purchase for inventory can depend on

A marketing forecast
The existing inventory levels
The rate of inventory usage
The availability of vendor material
Warehousing facilities/costs
Financial availability
Transport costs/time

The decision complexities and business rule dependencies are far beyond the mental capabilities of business operatives. If the business operatives are working under differing or conflicting sets of rules, chaos prevails. Everyone may believe he or she is doing the correct thing. Collectively, everyone may be acting in a manner that is counterproductive to the global interest.

Rule bottlenecks are exposed when personnel shifts take place or as isolated software packages silently superimpose their rules on a business department.

When mainstream information is provided for only a single process through a *separate application,* none of the business stewards can see the total effect or work together. Power politics can easily supplant group productivity. All business rules must be defined, integrated, indexed, and exposed.

Some process rules may be clear to some individuals but may be obscure to those with less experience. Business rules are frequently affected by

1. Strategy changes
2. Organization changes
3. Volume changes
4. Product introductions and changes
5. Business location changes
6. Customer service changes
7. External organization rules
8. Economics/cost change
9. The introduction of new technology

Business profits are affected adversely by uncoordinated reactions to the preceding changes.

For all of the preceding reasons, each of the business processes must be uniquely described in order to integrate all of them more tightly and to examine their interactive rules.

The integration of business processes is accomplished by knowing what information and what rules commonly apply to them. A visual display of process interaction is crucial to the integration. This display is accomplished by relating each process to its rules and to its elements (Chapter 4).

Managers must demand to see rule relationships in a consistent and architected way to be assured that business operatives are very clear in how the company is to operate.

To understand these relationships more clearly, the components of business processes may be analyzed at successive levels of detail using systems architecture. It is therefore necessary to know how systems architecture is constructed. Business systems need to be decomposed to understand how component changes effect each other.

A business system is a related set of functions and activities involving interactive rules that create integrated information and that use information to meet business objectives.

When information describing business processes is not highly structured and integrated, the detail is overwhelming and cannot be pursued logically.

BUSINESS SYSTEM ARCHITECTURE (CONSTRUCTION)

Defining Business Activities and Functions

It is clear that business information and automation planning requires much more detail than that described by only naming business processes. The business process must be architected to lower levels of detail.

Business operatives within each business process are engaged in two classes of work:

1. Activities (mental work)
2. Functions (physical work)

An activity.   An activity is related to human thinking, reasoning, rule formulation, and decision making. Knowledge workers perform activities when they plan, analyze, evaluate, measure, and diagnose the progress of the business. Knowledge about activities is required in order to verify that business operatives are engaged in productive mental work. Mental work is the equivalent of the "right side of the brain." Four out of five workers are engaged in knowledge activities.

A function.   A function takes place when a repetitive set of physical tasks is performed according to preset rules. Clerical staffs are normally thought to be performing functions when they file data, run machines, record events, or engage in routine physical work. This physical work is the equivalent of the "left side of the human brain." One out of five workers is engaged in physical- (production-) type work.

This distinction may appear to be inconsequential in initiating a knowledge architecture. However, both activities and functions are costs to the business and must be measured. The functional side of human work traditionally is where most computer automation projects begin and end. Human functions are sometimes replaced by computer functions one for one. Cost may be reduced. Innovation may not be improved. In these cases, there is little change in perception gears.

Automating the functions of business information handlers has saved many direct payroll/benefit dollars. Functions are expressed as a command verb followed by a subject term string, for example,

COMMAND VERB	MAJOR SUBJECT
[Record]	[Customer sales orders]
[Enter]	[Product reservations]
[Prepare]	[Payroll checks]
[Grant]	[Customer credit authorization]
[Produce]	[Product shipment documents]
[Record]	[Vendor purchase order receipts]
[Match]	[Vendor invoices] to [Company purchase orders]
[Validate]	[Product status]
[Update]	[Customer account balances]

Many business operatives and some management staff are exclusively involved in spreadsheet-type function work. The distinction between work functions and work activities is parallel to that of

1. Designing a machine (activity) [knowledge workers]
2. Operating a machine (function) [information handlers]

The major business advantages in the use of computerized automation are yet to be realized as human mental work is converted to machine functions.

Figure 5.4 displays a fragmentation of the business process. Both functions and activities interact and incur a cost to the enterprise. They must be measured in terms of their added value or cost to the business.

Frequently, business activity is given only cursory attention. This may be attributed to the political network within the work organization. Business operatives tend to transfer decisions/problems to others lest the power status quo be disturbed. Many middle managers prolong careers by invoking reports even after the responsibility for their decision is lost.

Any time that the human analysis can be functionally described, it can be transformed from an activity to a lower-cost automated function.

How many times do companies perform surveys or hire consultants to find out what the business functions are but seldom determine what information exists? How information is used, how decisions are made, why they are needed, or who makes them seem of little consequence. Millions of dollars are spent by corporations to teach consultants the functions of the business so they can propose fragmented and functional automation.

FIGURE 5.4   Business work process decomposition.

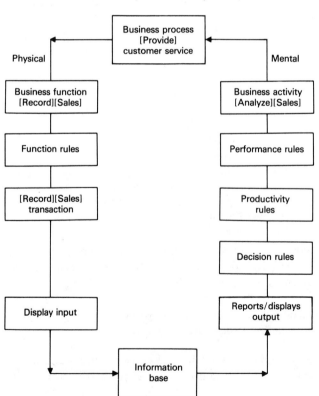

As a company becomes more highly automated, the obvious questions must be

What is all of the information produced used for?
What decisions are made?
What rules are invoked that should be changed?

Most functional information is actually used by business operatives to slow down the rate of their sequential functions. For example, a purchasing manager must examine all purchase order terms and the register summary before they are released to vendors.

Time after time, studies are not documented in a standard format. Little attention is given to keeping information resources up-to-date as a training tool or to keep up with what business rules are still current as business changes take place. The manager's mind is too fragile a storage device for it to be entrusted with the major knowledge of the business.

Few suggestions seem to arise regarding profit-making information overlaps between functions/activities because so much time is required to repeatedly define what currently exists in one format after another.

To pursue the value and interaction of business functions and activities, a common denominator for describing and connecting them must be used. That common standard is the system architecture. The system architecture is a part of the business knowledge directory that enables information about all work units to be accessed using a common information architecture.

The first step in architecting a system is to uniformly name all of the functions and activities so that information about them can be accessed and compared. The BKA context of consistent and meaningful names facilitates these associations.

Naming Business Work

Some business models have no standards for identifying or naming work subjects of the business. BKA systems architecture requires that discrete *names* be assigned to business activities and functions.

Business activities and functions have their origin in the BOT organization type described in Chapter 4. To establish consistency, the name of each activity and function of the business must take its name from one or more major subjects.

The major distinction in the name of a work object is that it must be modified by a control verb name to designate different types of work.

Within the verb type terms, it is necessary to differentiate between (1) physical-type verbs and (2) analytical/mental-type verbs, for example,

FUNCTION (PHYSICAL) VERBS	ACTIVITY (MENTAL) VERBS
REC.Record	PLN.Plan
PFR.Perform	ORG.Organize

FUNCTION (PHYSICAL) VERBS	ACTIVITY (MENTAL) VERBS
MOV.Move	MEA.Measure
VAL.Validate	ANL.Analyze
UPD.Update	SEL.Select
PRC.Process	MGT.Manage
SUM.Summarize	BGT.Budget

The distinction between physical and mental verbs is not always easy to perceive. The number of verbs needed to name all of the business activities and functions will be reasonably small and will not expand beyond a finite limit.

> Business work knowledge management requires a standard naming discipline.

The names of subjects within their type can be used in conjunction with command verbs to identify work activity and functions:

ACTIVITY NAMES

[CVT]	[BMT] MEASUREMENTS	[CVT]	[BRT] RESOURCES
[Measure]	[Sales]	[Analyze]	[Customers]
[Plan]	[Purchases]	[Select]	[Vendors]
[Control]	[Inventory]	[Price]	[Product]

FUNCTION NAMES

[CVT]	[BTT] TRANSACTIONS	[CVT]	[BRT] RESOURCES
[Record]	[Sales order]	[Invoice]	[Customer]
[Receive]	[Purchase order]	[Pay]	[Vendor]
[Pick]	[Product]	[Pack]	[Shipment]

From the examples, it should be clear that the use of subject types can control a diversity that might otherwise exist. Work can thus be identified and sorted into like types of work and be joined, retrieved, or compared using common subjects.

Appropriate naming helps to visually display where like types of work can be combined or associated. The use of a subject type name helps to show the relationships between information types: transactions, reports, tables, and files associated with any work type.

Work type directories are an important part of knowledge resource management. Information about work types is frequently missed in systems studies where standard object names are not used.

Many business models or business system studies terminate with the construction of a function flowchart that merely displays the sequence of the work. If a function-to-function sequence analysis is omitted, the result is usually the creation of another system very much like the existing one.

Where a business seeks to preserve its knowledge base, all of the relationships of work functions to other work functions must be maintained in order to evaluate the effect of any planned change. One of the most important object relationships of the work type is the business rule that governs it. Figure 5.5 displays a work decomposition required in order to identify and build reusable mini-functions which can be automated.

Business rule types are as follows:

Business Rule Types
1. Measurement rules, BMR
2. Organization rules, BOR
3. Location rules, BLR
4. Resource rules, BRR
5. Transaction rules, BTR
6. Product rules, BPT

Business rules are classified very much like business subjects. The BKA rule types are a convenient way to classify kinds of rules by the type of subject to which the rule relates.

Each company may create its own rule types and then proceed to associate its rules to their corresponding work. All rules, irrespective of their type, are expressed using, first, the command verb name (CVU) followed by its major business subject (object).

FIGURE 5.5   Business work function decomposition. Business work can be fragmented to any number of levels, and functions must be assigned sequence numbers.

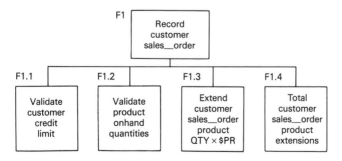

To convey the BKA rule type naming relationship, it is important to exemplify the expressions and relationships of rules to work and rules to information. Figure 5.6 depicts the levels of business rules: types, names, attributes, relationships.

After all of the business processes, activities, and functions are named, defined, and related, it is necessary to attach the *business work rules* that relate to each of them.

Figure 5.7 indicates that for each business function or activity, one or more business rules need to be associated with functions, activities, transactions, reports, displays, files, and tables.

Each of the business functions or activities has rules that pace the rate of the business cycle. Rules are the *core* of a business system.

Frequently, business rules are developed over time. Few may know what they are, why they exist, where they originate, how they relate, or if they integrate. "That's the way it's always been" is a remark that seems to perpetuate the status quo. Productivity is impeded by poorly structured rules or simply the inability to find and relate them to work or to information.

If the business rules are not relationally named, classified, and reviewed, they may never be challenged until a problem arises. Some business rules may have been prescribed to fit the sequence of the way things were done manually. They may have long since outlived their usefulness.

With the introduction of computer technology, it may have seemed natural to carry forward rules of manual mode into computer programs that often guarantee their perpetuity. No one argues with the computer! If

FIGURE 5.6   Business rule levels. Rule names belong to major rule types. Rule names are constructed using command verbs, subjects, and terms. The uniform use of object (subject) names facilitates the references between rules, work, and information. Rule units have their own attributes that append to their names and indicate properties.

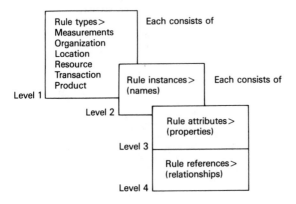

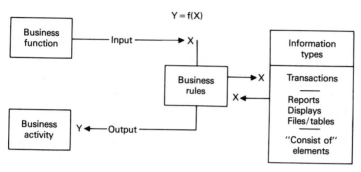

FIGURE 5.7   Business rules and information relationships. Business rules relate and join business information elements with business functions that create transactions or with business activities that require information. The mathematical expression is $Y = f(X)$, where Y is the output, X is the input, and (f) is the business rule that joins them.

you want to understand or change a computer rule, the chances are you'll be retired before it's on the agenda. Once the complexity becomes locked in computer code, there is little time for most business operatives to understand rule relationships.

Managers are seldom involved in the business/computer rule problem when competition is low and no customer complains about "delivery" once per week. Today, the customer shops the competitor with the minimum time delivery rule. When business rules are not continuously exposed and evaluated, no one thinks of the potential impact that one business rule has on another.

To compare like rules, an architecture of common names is required. If a rule is in the computer, it may be haphazardly mixed among hundreds of other rules. The change of a single rule can take a whole computer system down for weeks in rework when few know where all of the related rules are used. Conflicting rules may operate side by side, unnoticed for years.

Dusty procedure manuals may contain some rules, but few people will take the time to search them out for review.

An example of a business rule is the mechanism used to calculate an inventory reorder quantity. This rule is frequently referred to as the EOQ. An inventory systems manager of a major company responds that he does not know how the EOQ replenishment is calculated. He is too busy to find out. His response is "Why worry about it?" No one complains, and no documentation describes it. The systems manager does not know how to read the computerized code he was charged with controlling. The CEO frequently asks why inventory levels are so high, turnover low, and profit margins down. Inventory managers are too busy programming personal computers rather than evaluating rule relationships.

The data processing director is busy installing additional computer hardware to store more years of inventory history. No one may be contesting how the existing computer rules are affecting the total business. Is there time to find out? The robot has won again because the whole system is too disorganized and complex for any one individual to comprehend which business rules relate to which functions and activities.

The challenge of the situation is to name and organize the business rules so that they can be related and analyzed. If business rules are not uniformly identified, then any single rule change can involve changing a single rule in hundreds of computer programs only as each discrepancy or error is detected.

The rules in a business can number in the thousands. They can have a high degree of volatility. If they are organized by subject type and named using standard subject names, they can at least be accessed and compared systematically. If the rule organization project is not given top priority, then business managers can be expected to fight fire after fire with no end in sight. It is common sense to name, relate, and organize the rules that drive the business. Rules may be stated at a very high level or at a very detailed level.

The ability to quickly change business rules in one place and have them apply to all business processes simultaneously gives any business a highly competitive advantage. To facilitate control, the following must occur:

1. Meaningful names must be assigned to business rules.
2. The business rules must be related to all of the business functions and subjects to which they apply.
3. A standard method for rule expression must be selected.

A standard method of business rule construction is required.

BUSINESS RULE CONSTRUCTION

Business rules consist of two major segments:

1. Action segment
2. Condition segment

The action segment consists of three parameters:

1. RUL_CVN.Command verb (operator) name
2. RUL_OBN.Object (operand) name
3. RUL_LMT.Limitation (range)

The condition segment consists of three parameters:

1. RUL_SBJ.Subject
2. RUL_OPR.Comparator
3. RUL_VAL.Value

Several condition segments may relate to each action segment. Many action segments may relate to a condition segment. A rule will "fire" when all of its associated segment conditions are met. Where rules are named using BKA standards, like type rules can be selected from a rule name list, using either the command verb name, the rule object (subject) name, or the combination. Rule examples are appropriate for displaying the rule naming and construction concept. Figure 5.8 depicts the major segments of business rules. Figure 5.9 depicts the encapsulated segments which need to be identified, created, and updated for each business rule.

Each condition of a rule is expressed as a subject-attribute-value combination element. Each action of a rule is expressed as a subject-attribute-value element coupled to a command verb unit.

Multiple conditions can exist for a single action. Multiple actions can exist for a single condition, and multiple conditions can exist for multiple actions.

FIGURE 5.8 Rule segments.

Action segment

Command verb	Object	Limiter instance

Condition (if/where) segment

Subject	Condition	Value

Measurement type rule

Maintain $ cost	Inventory	First in, first out

Product	Equal to, =	Engines

Organization type rule

Create	District	New

Sales	Greater than, >	$100,000

Location type rule

Ship from	City	Chicago

Product quantity	Less than, <	10,000 units

Resource type rule

Select	Carrier	Truck

Distance	Less than, <	150 miles

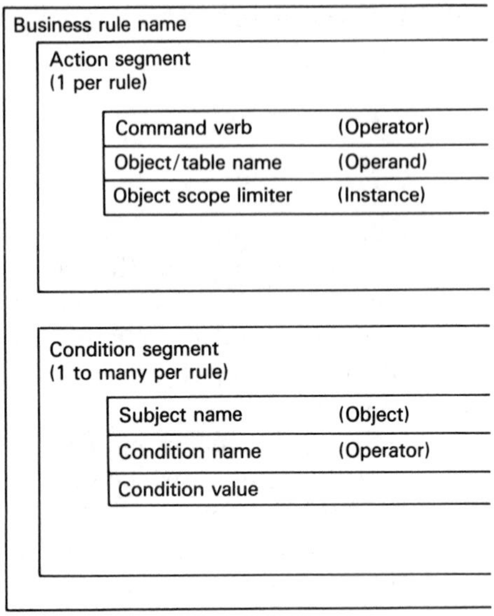

Business rule name	
Action segment (1 per rule)	

Command verb	(Operator)
Object/table name	(Operand)
Object scope limiter	(Instance)

Condition segment (1 to many per rule)	

Subject name	(Object)
Condition name	(Operator)
Condition value	

FIGURE 5.9   Business rule encapsulation.

A business rule may relate to many business processes or to only specific business functions or activities. The rules must be tightly structured using their related expressions and major business subject to simplify their meanings.

When business rules are *named* using a subject/subject combination as the key index, they can be accessed, evaluated, and compared quickly relative to their impact on the profit calculation. Conversely, if the rules are not named consistently, they cannot be easily found, reviewed, or compared to the subjects or to the work functions to which they apply. Business rules are named using both the command verb and its object name as a combination.

> Knowledge architecture requires a method to integrate, relate, and index business rules.

Summary

In summary, all business rules must be named. They must be grouped by rule type and placed in object name sequence. Business knowledge architecture allows for this structuring but cannot guarantee that the rules will be architected or named correctly.

The rules are the drivers for the computer programs discussed in the next section of this chapter. Computer software rules can be controlled if their related business rules can be identified, related, and integrated.

Business rule standardization requires an extensive analysis of detail. Since a single rule can be responsible for thousands of dollar profits, the control cost is well worth the verification effort. The cost of rule analysis is substantially reduced when it is undertaken in a methodical way by major subject.

A computerized tool can be used to name, index, store, and access the business rules but only after naming standards are created and a name is applied to each rule. The volume of rules and rule changes is simply too large to attempt business rule control with manual methods. Many organizations persist in addressing business rules in an ad hoc way until they are knocked out by competitors who have implemented rule identification, standardization, and review techniques.

Business rules can be controlled using computer software. A computerized tool can access definitions and relationships of business rules that apply to work functions and information usage.

> Business knowledge architecture is a method used to display business work and rule relationships.

KNOWLEDGE SOFTWARE ARCHITECTURE

If information architecture is a standard framework for naming and organizing data and systems architecture organizes work processing and rules related to that work, then software architecture is a standard mechanism to create, control, and maintain computer jobs\programs\ modules\rules.

An executive may ask "Do I really need to know all of this?" The answer is "Yes!," at least from a planning view point, which this book addresses. For too long executives have been shielded from the detail required to understand and control computerized business knowledge. Consequently, they have not put forth the necessary funds to permanently identify, protect and implement the company information resource investment.

By 1990, every bright college senior will have a good perspective of how a computer system works. Their primary question will be "What is the status of the company business knowledge base?" The best will not be impressed by

1. Piecemeal data processing projects
2. A particular type of computer hardware
3. Specific programming languages/packages

They will try to avoid a company that is in chaos with its computerized data. After all, why pursue a career rearranging data, again and again, for a management that doesn't know the difference? Automated reasoning systems are where careers are to be made. The automation of decisions relies on the ability to recognize, relate, and maintain uniform data definitions.

By 2001, today's software capability will look like Model T Fords. While computer hardware and communications architecture will dramatically advance cost/performance using parallel processing, only knowledge architecture can provide the gearbox needed to utilize it for better profits. Spreadsheets 100 miles long and 200 miles deep will not do the job. The knowledge asset will be more important than the new plant or office site. Therefore, it is in our best interest to explore

1. What knowledge software is
2. What knowledge software must do
3. How knowledge software must be controlled

Computer hardware, communications, and software are rapidly becoming more independent and substitutable, and they are expected to be relational and connectable. The investment in software is accumulating and can no longer be viewed as short-term (throw-away) parts. Software is no longer exclusively the domain of data processing technicians. If the proper software is created as a foundation, it can be expected to be modular and expansible and to last over a long period of time, even with changes in business needs and computer technology.

BKA* software is a tool for integrating knowledge rules and information for long-term company profit-making strategy. If piecemeal, personalized data identification is allowed, the entire company can become mired forever in computer software structural problems rather than profit-making ventures.

One of the most important perspectives for senior management is the information architecture, which was discussed in previous chapters. The strategic perspective of how the company organizes data is identified as business information architecture.

The principle of computer software architecture is similar to that in many other scientific structures. If the basic elements of the business functions are factored to their lowest common denominator, then both information and rules can be reassembled within a total company information platform.

Modular computer software can be created to be very similar to the chemical table of elements. If basic particle characteristics are identified, their compounds can be constructed and repetitively utilized. This same principle applies to the elements of computerized business knowledge.

Once a word string formula is constructed, it is not necessary to rename it, only to control it.

Some years ago, the use of the telephone became so voluminous that forecasts indicated that half of the people in the United States would have to become telephone switchboard operators. Consequently, Bell Laboratories invented the user-based automatic dial system. This transferred the dialing function directly to the telephone user by providing a simple *standard* dialing technique.

The situation in computer system productivity has a parallel to the telephone dilemma; however, the dispersal of work to the business operative (via the PC) is not following any data standard, such as the automatic dialer device. Different vendors, hardware, languages, networks, protocols, names, and nomenclatures are dispersing the available talent, rather than increasing human productivity. The result is an increase in the frequency of wrong numbers and lost time in information acquisition.

Computer industry vendors are moving to what is called *open system architecture* (a way to standardize or connect various types of computer hardware and software). IBM has named their standardized hardware connection/migration technique systems application architecture (SAA).

These technical efforts should not be confused by business managers with specific business applications, even though vendors may imply some application magic exists by the names of their software products. The goal of these types of products is to connect different types of hardware and to provide data communication hardware/software standards.

While hardware and software standards will yield substantial cost savings for computer vendors, a parallel standard for work, rule, and information controls, as described in this book, is needed for business organizations.

The hardware or software developed in the data processing evolution has been responsible for the creation and usage of many proprietary standards that are meant to improve group profitability and productivity of the business.

The concept of reusable computer software architecture has been perceived as a needed standard for controlling and improving computer software. The objectives are clear, but the means of transition are unclear. Software architecture objectives:

1. Manage complexity of the data processing environment
2. Increase the productivity and lower the cost of staff resources
3. Shift business rule changes to business operatives
4. Improve data services by fast change modular capability
5. Move into a real-time information display and job assistance mode
6. Facilitate planning, management, control, and measurement
7. Use the computer to manage its own complexity
8. Direct automation spending toward integrated architectural business standards

Computer Software Integration

Application software is an area in need of standards. However, application software responsibility has been primarily that of the department using it. Software architecture is primarily a standard way of integrating functions to interact with business information and rules. Figure 5.10 depicts a high-level view of a platform structure that any computer system documentation can address. Computer software architecture maintains a uniform and identical perspective for the processing of data directly from and to all of the business processes.

Figure 5.10 is a composite that depicts how business activities are related by transaction to seven computer master functions. Any business process computer cycle can be depicted using this identical format. Pages of diverse system flow diagrams can be replaced using standard computerized transaction diagrams and views. The standard view requires a change of perspective from the traditional function-to-function flowchart.

A classification of master computer functions serves as a visual guide for management to use to validate transaction processing rules on a function-by-function basis by each incoming transaction. A more detailed

FIGURE 5.10   Computer software architecture.

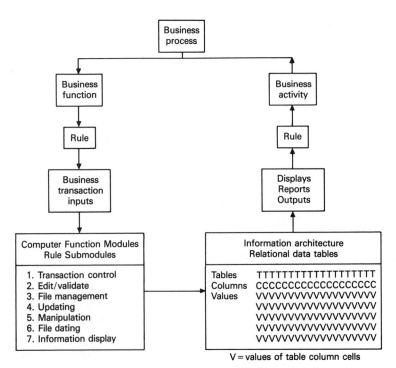

description of computer software functions may help to demonstrate the advantages of this modular view.

Computer Function Type

Figure 5.11 is another view of the master computer functions that any computer executes when it relates and joins the business transactions generated by business functions to and from the information base.

Computerized master functions are primarily activated by business transactions, for example, the sales order and its elements:

INFORMATION ELEMENTS	VALUE
Transaction control IDN	1234
Transaction account IDN	122-23
Transaction type identifier	Sales return
Organization department	Sales department
Customer IDN	43212
Company location IDN	Chi-34
Product IDN	Kludge #45
Product $/price	$10.00
Product unit	Each
Product quantity	4
Tax rate	7%
Date	12-25-88
Time of day	132412
Originator	Smith

FIGURE 5.11   Computer function archetype.
NOTE: Information views are used by computer master functions to join, relate, project, and control business system input transactions and output displays.

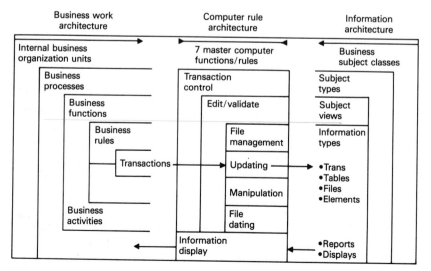

Any business transaction can have multiple elements, each with associated computer rules to govern how all transaction elements are to be processed. In any business there can be hundreds of different transactions and rules.

Computer function architecture identifies and accesses business transactions and combines them by the computer function required to process them.

Computer master functions (CMFs) are high-level classifications of computer work rules. They are a way to organize all computer rules so that they can be retrieved, examined, and reused.

Computer function rules are an extension of business rules and interact with the company information. There is a need to name computer rules in a standard BKA so that computer programmers and business operatives can retrieve and understand what the programs are doing. If computer rules are decomposed and categorized as part of the total infrastructure,

1. Overall complexity can be reduced.
2. Redundancy and rule conflict can be minimized.
3. Reusable computer code can be created and reused.

Computer Function Classifications

The seven computer master functions are named and numbered as follows:

1. Transaction control
2. Edit/validate
3. File management
4. Updating
5. Manipulation
6. File dating
7. Information display

1. Transaction control. Transaction control consists of all of the subfunctions that are related to successfully recording an event of the business. The event record itself is called a transaction. A transaction is a collection of data elements that are logically grouped together when recording a business event. Transaction control is a set of subfunctions that are invoked to process all of the elements of a transaction. These subfunctions

1. Identify the transaction using master transaction tables
2. Authorize the transaction for admittance to the system
3. Count and sequence the transaction admitted

4. Date the transaction
5. Establish a value of the transactions admitted
6. Identify/relate the transaction to a person/location
7. Control the format of the transaction
8. Control the protocols of the transaction

2. Edit/validate.   Edit/validate consists of all the subfunctions (rules) that are related to ensuring that each data element value in a transaction is accurate, complete, and consistent.

Edit consists of the subfunctions (rules) related to a data element itself. Edit exists when

1. All required data elements of the transaction are accounted for and related.
2. Each required data element is characterized/signed accurately.

Validate consists of the subfunctions (rules) that compare each data element to a prestored file value. Validation exists when

1. All data elements of the transaction are related to or compared to their counterparts of a file.
2. All data elements are related to rules of comparison.
3. All data elements are related to other elements of the transaction.

Note: All business transactions and their elements are controlled by both transaction control and edit/validate functions before they are passed to the remaining five functions.

3. File management.   File management consists of all of the subfunctions required for a transaction that creates, updates, or deletes a record type or element space in a file or table. File management does not process the content or value of the spaces. File management subfunctions include the following:

1. Specify names of data, record, file spaces/partitions
2. Create sizes of data, record, file spaces/partitions
3. Specify locations for data, record, file spaces
4. Assign physical devices for data, record, file spaces
5. Control counts and sizes of records/file spaces
6. Relate files to files, records to records, elements to elements, and tables to tables

4. Updating.   Updating consists of all of the subfunctions (rules) required for a transaction that requires the accumulation of its quantifiable content and value. The posting function specifies the following:

1. Post data to specific data elements
2. Add new data content value to existing data content

3. Delete or subtract data content from existing contents
4. Replace existing data content with new data content

5. Manipulation.   Manipulation consists of subfunctions (rules) required for a transaction to process previously stored data. The implied rules relate to a specific transaction. Processing specifies the following:

1. Perform calculations using data
2. Add, subtract, multiply, and divide
3. Execute algorithms/formulas
4. Perform posting of changed data

6. File dating.   File dating consists of subfunctions that utilize a time transaction to separate files by time periods. File dating specifies the following:

1. Date files
2. Perform time period accumulations of data, records, files
3. Maintain record and file counts by time period
4. Open new files and extensions

7. Information display.   Information display consists of subfunctions that withdraw data and format reports from existing files according to each report transaction rule. The information display function specifies the following:

1. VDT display output formats
2. Report formats/summaries
3. Report transmissions and formats
4. Printed reports and video displays

Why are these computer master functions and their rules important? The master functions ensure that transaction data of any business process are uniformly controlled element by element. Traditionally, computer function logic is duplicated in system after system, package after package, program after program, and file after file, increasing system development and operations time.

If the master functions are put in place modularly, the control modules can be programmed one time and the computer program logic used repeatedly, not re-created. Any single business transaction can require the execution of one or more of the computer master functions and many subfunctions. Ensuring that all of the related transaction components are concurrently and completely processed is referenced as principle of "1" (no further processing of a transaction is needed).

The seven master functions group computer program subfunctions by type of control and provide the first step in modularization. They are named and indexed identically to business rules.

Traditionally, computer functions have been fragmented to modify multiple independent data files. They are frequently programmed multiple times and staged and processed sequentially, which results in very high programmer productivity losses, time lags, and more operational costs than necessary. Data is frequently staged to update one set of information files after another.

The updating frequency can be stretched over a long period of time and over multiple programs, which lowers the value and usability of the information itself.

The prime objective of the master functions is to ensure that the transaction is completely posted to every part of the infrastructure immediately as it is received (the principle of "1"). A single transaction may not appear to be significant. Its cumulative effect on the company information accuracy can be significant. Holding back parts and pieces of a transaction for more efficient computer usage was a necessary strategy with slower technology; for the parallel computer technology of the 1990s, a sequential updating strategy is no longer valid.

The systems of today frequently duplicate or mix the computer master functions. As this happens, the add-on subsystems become more complex, and maintenance costs skyrocket. When a simple change is needed, the time and people training to find all of the modules for change takes more time. Testing the systems takes longer to ensure that the change did not disturb other parts of the larger system. If the transactions are grouped and controlled by master function modules, changes in logic need not require entire system program rewrites or replacements. Software investments are then protected.

Businesses usually do not explore the reduced development costs that can result from transaction-oriented modularization. Reusable code is not a new concept to sophisticated software vendors or those specializing in computer software operating systems and data base utilization.

The term *system* can best be used to reference a global context rather than a single application. Business process modules that consist of standardized transaction and computer functions will eventually replace the disjointed *application orientation* of today.

The user system interface display must be able to reference globally any component of the business system using a single and integrated information work station. It must encompass the business view, logical view, and physical view as a single context. Multiple-tier architectures simply require too much translation time, too much cost, too many gurus, and too much management confusion.

SUMMARY

It is appropriate to recapitulate what has been described as the basic parts of business knowledge. The following categories were established to simplify and modularize a business knowledge infrastructure:

Knowledge domains: Identify strategic bodies of business knowledge

Subject types and terminology types: Establish and prioritize and restrict subjects that are used to name and relate all knowledge units of the company

Information types: Standard categories used to classify and cluster data; reports, files, displays, transactions, tables

Work types: Organize and relate business processes, activities, and functions of the business

Rule types: Organize and relate business and computer rules of the business

More organizations have not standardized components of information in a relational way. Many companies have only a minimum level of basic data standards or nomenclature. The fine edge of productivity cannot be honed without highly structured information standards as the basis for rule definitions.

Without a BKA type of architecture, the use of computerized technology will increase complexity rather than simplify the business cycle. Power domain conflicts (created by complexity) can only be disarmed by simplifying and exposing how all system components must interact.

The global system subjects and terms are the lowest common building blocks (denominators) of business knowledge architecture. They must be engineered, related, and controlled if a business knowledge project is to bring about group understanding and productivity. Table 5.1 depicts the levels of business subject and terminology and their corresponding levels of work and rule organization.

Table 5.1   BKA* Work and Rule Architecture (Levels)

Knowledge Levels	Business Work/Rules				
	Encyclopedia		Work and Rule Inventory		
1. Category	Business subject category	Business terminology category	Business work category	Business rule category	The highest level of work/rule knowledge encapsulation
2. Type	Subject types	Term types	Work types	Rule types	Knowledge types classify like kinds of work and rules

Table 5.1   BKA* Work and Rule Architecture (Levels) (cont.)

Knowledge Levels	Business Work/Rules				
	Encyclopedia		Work and Rule Inventory		
	Subject	Term	Work	Rule	
3. Unit-name table	Subject unit-names	Term unit-names	Work unit-names	Rule unit-names	Member unit-name that belongs to its knowledge type
4. Unit attribute column	Subject attributes	Term attributes	Work attributes	Rule attributes	Extensions of units using their unique attributes
5. Unit references	Subject references	Term references	Work references	Rule references	Type\unit to type\unit binding
6. Unit statements	Subject statements	Term statements	Work statements	Rule statements	Text statements

1. Business *subjects* establish a global naming hierarchy for constructing work and rule names.
2. Business *terms* provide extensions and limitations for uniform and unique work and rule names.
3. Work and rule names are constructed using only subject names and term extensions.

Chapter 6

Knowledge Integration

INTRODUCTION

Business knowledge invokes action, and business action requires information.

Business profits and productivity are a function of how effectively the preceding subjects are synchronized and integrated.

The lack of a single interrelated view can cause needless translations, confusion, duplication, delays, and unnecessary costs. Only a few businesses are using a global or integrated strategy in planning their information or systems.

The benefits of consistent business knowledge architecture (BKA) are not immediately obvious. Some managers have a complete disregard for information organization as a project. The obsession of business managers with computer hardware, package software, and network technology as a panacea for group productivity can easily obscure the potential benefits of information integration. Frequently, technologies are not utilized to their full potential because they require specialized techniques and training to exploit them. Business knowledge architecture is one such technique.

Previous chapters have identified business knowledge representations for the following:

Business work types
Business rule types
Business information types

The purpose of establishing these domains is to provide a uniform architecture to identify and organize their subjects using consistent semantics and syntax.

However, the overriding objective is to allow all BKA subjects of any domain to be integrated so that any subject of one type can be quickly related to subjects of any other type without complex translations. Profitable action can then be quickly identified.

Disjointed information is one of the most serious inhibitors of business knowledge preservation and productivity. Disorganized business information proliferates because a BKA "superrelativity" context for business knowledge has not been introduced. Without a global context, business subject interaction cannot be observed. Without a knowledge of subject interaction, profits fail to materialize.

If business *excellence* or *productivity* objectives are ever to be achieved, their roots must begin with understanding how business knowledge can be created, updated, integrated, and accessed using computer-assisted technology. Business knowledge integration needs to be defined.

What does BKA integration mean?
When any work, rule, and information subject of the business knowledge domain can be related to any other subject using the same standards, semantics, and syntax without duplication, then integration exists.

BUSINESS KNOWLEDGE DOMAINS

A view of BKA knowledge infrastructure levels is found in Figure 6.1. The graphic displays the symmetry of the business knowledge domains.

1. *The work image* categorizes business action/work and its levels and rules.
2. *The rule image* categorizes business rules by subject type priority.
3. *The info image* categorizes business information and its abstract levels of detail.

For each domain there are corresponding levels of object specificity. Business knowledge levels integrate and relate work, rule, and information type relationships at five respective levels.

These relationships can be mechanized using standard word geometry to link work/rule/information subject context from high levels to detail levels.

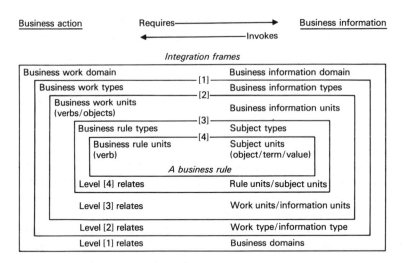

FIGURE 6.1   Business knowledge domain (encapsulation).

Subject key names index and relate both business actions/rules with their corresponding levels of information. Any two categories can be related at their corresponding level. The levels converge to discrete business rules.

High-level business objectives and goals relate to work functions that are identified using related subject names.

Similarly, as business action prescriptions are established, corresponding information pattern matches must be extended to lower levels. If common work and information are not related, using like word geometry, communication becomes cluttered with loosely connected ideas, and overall productivity slips. When the context from high-level abstractions to low-level detail information is not linked, human chaos prevails.

A seamless gearbox of relational nomenclature can provide a clear transition between ideas.

BUSINESS KNOWLEDGE INFRASTRUCTURE

The number of business subject relationships that can exist may appear to be infinite. However, careful classification, indexing, and name selection can dramatically reduce the number of work, rule, and information units as well as restrict the number of relationships needed for a global integration.

From previous chapters, it is clear that *vertical* integration exists within domain types when

1. Work types consist of lower-level work instances
2. Rule types consist of lower-level rule instances
3. Info types consist of lower-level info instances

Vertical integration of each type depends on and is facilitated by the standard use of BKA domain type priority and the uniform subject/term (access name) abbreviations, previously described in Chapters 4 and 5. These subject/term combinations are intratype relationships because they

1. Focus on a view within a single domain type
2. Reference subjects within the *same* domain type

Figure 6.2 depicts the three BKA domain types and their levels. The *horizontal* integration between any two domain types is accomplished using two levels of identification:

1. Subject type to subject type (type relationship)
2. Subject to subject (subject relationship)

To simplify and limit the number of relationships needed between business subjects, the BKA relationship types are restricted to six directional combinations.

FIGURE 6.2 Business knowledge infrastructure, global domain. BKA integration is achieved using like subject key access abbreviations. BKA references are minimized by restricting the number of reference paths:

1. Work type/unit to work type/unit references
2. Work type/unit to rule type/unit references
3. Work type/unit to info type/unit references
4. Rule type/unit to rule type/unit references
5. Rule type/unit to info type/unit references
6. Info type/unit to info type/unit references

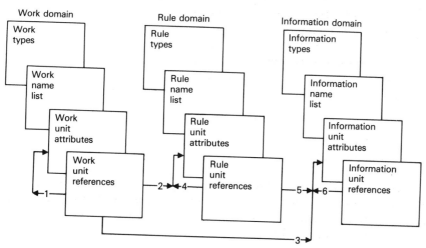

Three of the BKA relationships relate *within* their respective domains, and three of the BKA relationships relate *between* their respective domains as follows:

DOMAIN TYPE INTRARELATIONSHIPS

1. Work type to work type
4. Rule type to rule type
6. Info type to info type

DOMAIN TYPE INTERRELATIONSHIPS

2. Work type to rule type
3. Work type to info type
5. Rule type to info type

Respective instances of the preceding relationship types are then also limited by the six directional priorities, reducing the number of global instance combinations.

While the preceding BKA relationship rules require a margin of discipline, they in no way inhibit or restrict the construction of any relational expression.

The business manager is concerned with the ability to access knowledge by any subject type and its unit in the global business domain. Then the need is to continuously query for and track reference upon reference until the final question or answer is found.

The continuous query requires the facility to suspend source subjects while searching for referenced target subjects and then to make the target subject a source subject for yet another query for more target subjects. A reference trail is required to backtrack to previously selected subjects within the search path.

This process may initially sound complex; however, the preceding associative procedure is exactly how many executives think and perform on a day-to-day basis. The query difficulty is frequently found in the physical bulk and divergent names for graphics, reports, videotext, phone, E-mail, etc. The human limits of memory in putting it all together for a business decision can be a manager's nightmare.

The use of a BKA type-by-instance query facility can help focus and simplify the global query problem.

Figure 6.3 is an example of a global BKA schema for an associative information system. It is made up of business knowledge source types and relationship options. The diagonal array is partitioned by the BKA domains:

1. Work
2. Rules
3. Information

The diagonal array enables the source type to target type relationship to be stipulated using the symbol (>) to expose which knowledge relationships the business maintains. The reader may also note that the *hierarchy of types* is preserved within the respective domains.

		(Context)	(Acronym)
>	– Work domain (hierarchy) – – – – – – – – – – – – – – – – – –	(Global)	– – – – –
1	. . X Missions	(Business)	MIS
2	. > X Objectives	(Business)	OBJ
3	. . > X Goals	(Business)	GOL
4	. . . . > X Plans	(Business)	PLN
5	. . . . . > X Projects	(Business)	PRJ
6	. . . . . . > X Processes	(Business)	PRC
7	. . . . X Activities	(Employee)	ACT
8	. . . . > . X Functions	(Employee)	FNC
9	. . . . X Jobs	(Employee)	JOB
10	. . . . X Tasks	(Employee)	TSK
11	. . . . > . . . . . . X Computer/automated jobs	(Machine)	CJB
12	. . . . > X Computer programs	(Machine)	PRG
13	. . . . > X Computer program functions	(Machine)	CPF
14	. . . . X Computer program lines	(Machine)	CPL
>	– – – – – – – – – Rule domain (hierarchy) – – – – – – – – – –	(Global)	– – – – –
1	. . . . > . . . . > . . . . X Measurement rules	(Business)	MRT
2	. . . . . . > . . . . > . . . . . X Organization rules	(Business)	ORT
3	. . . . . . > . . : . . > . . . . . . X Location rules	(Business)	LRT
4	. . . . . . > . . . . > . . . . X Resource rules	(Business)	RRT
5	. . . . . . > . . . . > . . . . X Transaction rules	(Business)	TRT
6	. . . . . . > . . . . > . . . . X Product rules	(Business)	PRT
>	– – – – – – – – – – – – – Information domain (hierarchy) – – – – –	(Global)	– – – – –
1	. . . . > . . . . X Data bases	(Machine)	DBS
2	. . . . > . . . . X Data segments	(Machine)	DSG
3	. . . . > . . . . X Files (records)	(Machine)	FIL
4	. . . . > . . . . X Tables	(Machine)	TBL
5	. . . . > . . . . X Displays (VDT)	(Machine)	DST
6	. . . . > . . . . X Reports	(Machine)	RPT
7	. . . . > . . . . X Transactions (documents)	(Machine)	TRT
>	– – – – – – – – – – – – – – – Data dictionary _ _ _ _ _ _ _ _	(Global)	– – – – –
1	. . . . > > > > > > . . . . X Data elements	(Business)	ELE
2	. . . . > X Subjects	(Business)	SBJ
3	. . . . > X Terms	(Business)	TRM
>	– –		

FIGURE 6.3 Business knowledge integration (chart of accounts), domain type hierarchy and relationships. Each of the business knowledge domain source types forms a relationship type when it references a subordinate target type. The symbol used to show the source to target relationship is a ">." The domains have an implicit superior to subordinate direction in controlling knowledge architecture. Work/rule/info/data relationships are controlled within seven relationship types: work to work, work to rule, work to info, rule to rule, rule to info, info to info, info to data. Subjects and terms are the lowest level of information types. They are used to geometrically construct the names of all business object types.

Figure 6.3 is only a brief example of the relational array that will exist for a business enterprise if it is to integrate and control its global knowledge.

The idea behind the business knowledge architecture is to have a global framework to allow business managers access to all business knowledge domains and their interrelationships.

A business enterprise may choose many more information type relationships than those indicated. However, careful decisions are required regarding which subjects to control.

The following are a few selected global relationships that an enterprise may elect to maintain:

DOMAIN	RELATES TO	DOMAIN
Work	Relates to	Work
Projects	>	Computer jobs
Computer jobs	>	Computer programs
Computer programs	>	Computer functions
Work	Relates to	Rules
Business processes	>	Measurement rules
Business functions	>	Location rules
Computer programs	>	Transaction rules
Work	Relates to	Information
Business functions	>	Transactions
Computer programs	>	Tables
Computer programs	>	Reports
Computer programs	>	Displays (VDT)
Rule	Relates to	Information
Resource rules	>	Data elements
Product rules	>	Reports
Information	Relates to	Information
Reports	>	Data elements
Tables	>	Data elements
Displays	>	Data elements

It is not unusual for the business manager to require access to some of the preceding information relationships. Without a global architectural framework of existing knowledge and information, questions and answers can be very difficult to express and access. If the manager has to ask other managers or technicians to obtain information, the time lag in finding and producing results is too long.

Some typical queries are as follows:

1. Query all of the business rules that relate to sales and then query each rule definition.
2. Query all of the data elements (names) of a given report and then query each data element definition.
3. Query all computer programs containing a given rule and then query the corresponding data element definitions.
4. Query all of the transactions used in a business function and then query each transaction element definition.
5. Query all of the reports that relate to sales for a time period and then query sales by location for the same time period.
6. Query all of the business goals of a specific department and then query department projects leading to that goal.
7. Query all of the inventory rules for a class of product and then query each rule statement.

The relational view of Figure 6.3 is physically created as a set of tables. They are menus of domain types and their unit instances. The tables are part of a relational data base platform (RDBMS).

Table 6.1 is a global view of all of the frames that link the BKA domain types, instances, references, and statements. Using the BKA type data base, the business manager is able to initiate a global search for any subject or relationship within the knowledge base of the enterprise simply by selecting its type and its subject access name, for example,

1. Select any knowledge type by domain
2. Select a list of units by access name or by knowledge type
3. Select a unit and its attributes from the list of units
4. Select all relationships of the selected unit (domain type sequence)
5. Select the relationship's type and unit name as a source and repeat step 3.

Table 6.1 Business Knowledge Directory

Knowledge Levels	Encyclopedia		Knowledge Inventory			Definitions
1. Domain	Subject	Term	Work	Rule	Info	A classification of business knowledge areas
2. Type	Subject type	Term type	Work type	Rule type	Info type	Classifications of like business subjects
3. Unit-name	Subject name	Term name	Work name	Rule name	Info name	All instances of each domain type (table names)
4. Unit attribute (column)	Subject atr.	Term atr.	Work atr.	Rule atr.	Info atr.	Extensions of each unit-name
5. Unit reference	S/S	S/T T/T	W/W	W/R R/R	W/I R/I I/I	Type/unit to type/ unit relation- ships
6. Text	Subject text	Term text	Work text	Rule text	Info text	Business rule dec- larations and statements

1. These knowledge categories and levels are used to organize, express, and relate business work, rules, and information that refer to the same subject names.

2. The encyclopedia subjects and terms are used to uniformly construct the names of work, rules, and information.

3. Unit references only relate in a left to right direction in order to restrict the number of combinations, for example, (1) work relates to work, (2) work relates to rules, (3) work relates to info, (4) rules relate to rules, (5) rules relate to info, (6) info relates to info.

Selective queries can be made using the type/subject/term access names as search arguments.

A few examples of relational type-to-type/instance-to-instance BKA selections are appropriate:

SOURCE			RELATES TO >	TARGET
Domain	=	Work	>	Work
Type	=	Project (PRJ)	>	Computer job (CJB)
Name	=	Create vendor invoice	>	Extend vendor invoice
Access	=	[CRE] [VDR_IVC_PRJ]	>	[EXT] [VDR_IVC_CJB]
Domain	=	Work	>	Rule
Type	=	Business function (FNC)	>	Transaction rule (TRT)
Name	=	Enter customer sales orders	>	Validate customer $ credit
Access	=	[ETR] [CST_S/O_FNC]	>	[VLD] [CST_$CR_TRT]
Domain	=	Work	>	Information
Type	=	Computer program (PRG)	>	Report (RPT)
Name	=	Print sales month to date	>	Sales month to date
Access	=	[PRN] [SLS_MTD_PRG]	>	[SLS_MTD_RPT]
Domain	=	Information	>	Information
Type	=	Display (VDT)	>	Data element (ELE)
Name	=	Vendor invoice	>	Vendor ID number
Access	=	[VDR_IVC_VDT]	>	[VDR_IDN_ELE]

The preceding display shows how the type-to-type and instance-to-instance object relationships are actually maintained. The syntax for all domains is identical.

A distinction can be drawn between the search for knowledge (meta information) and content information. It is clear that initially the business manager needs access to what information is available; then immediate access the *content* of that same information is needed without a delay.

The BKA paradigm is required to focus and structure the thinking of the business manager regarding what information should be related and how to query it efficiently. The domain type and instance combination query using standard type/subject/term (access name) abbreviations facilitates the query speed and control over global knowledge.

Without the consistency of BKA type standards and relationships, can the business manager really make effective use of a business communications network? Can the chief information officer (CIO) or business managers actually believe they have business knowledge under control?

It is beyond the scope of this book to describe the workings of relational data bases. A significant point is that relational software tools do not guarantee a logically correct construction of business subject relationships. Only the business managers using BKA type architecture can increase the quality of the business knowledge.

Many computerized tools exist which can graphically and textually display relationships of business subjects. They increase the speed of access; however managers must first describe which subjects are worth relating.

> A hallmark of human intelligence is an ability to quickly combine information in new ways.

KNOWLEDGE TOOLS

The extent of integrated business knowledge construction demands the speed and power and control of computer technology. The number of business subjects, rules, relationships, and functions is too complex to maintain without automated help, consistent machine-enforced standards, a common infrastructure, an easy change facility, and fast access.

Methodologies abound in what is referred to as computer-aided software engineering (CASE). These tools are being constructed at an increasing rate by a variety of software vendors. Millions of dollars have already been spent and continue to be invested in hundreds of lines of software designed to give system developers and programmers greater productivity. Every phase of what is referred to as the system life cycle (SLC) is being given tools to facilitate user design and program coding. It is an attempt to automate automation.

It is important to understand that even with these tools the "wrong" information, systems, and rules can still be created, only faster. More accurate "packaged garbage" can still prevail. Many of these CASE packages are simply extensions of the way things are currently done manually with flowcharts and pencils. The tools do not guarantee that any new perceptions will occur.

Early marketing attempts of CASE software have found some business resistance to investing in high-priced information engineers and design tools, even as other companies accelerate their research in this new science.

CASE tool facilities can be classified as follows:

1. Work stations
2. Graphic software
3. Libraries
4. Encyclopedias
5. Design assistance
6. Program generation

Work stations.   Work stations allow designers and coders to see the same picture. They can share and view charts uniformly and change work without disrupting the whole of previous work. Standards are invoked allowing for a more disciplined interaction of documentation.

Graphics.   Graphics support front-end systems design charts, boxes, colors, lines, connectors, and symbolics. Productivity is enhanced by eliminating the redrawing of diagrams as work progresses and changes are needed.

Libraries.   Libraries store objectives, plans, goals, projects, and information to keep designers focused on the milestones of system development and to furnish an index to all work components.

Encyclopedias.   Encyclopedias store all of the definitions of information, work, and rule types as reusable modules to reduce redundancy, enhance accuracy, and enforce consistency.

Design assistance.   Design assistance tracks design connections, flaws, inconsistencies, and completeness that could reduce system performance.

Program generation.   Program generation translates designs/specifications into source/computer code and provides productivity.

The lack of knowledge expression standards is one of the last crucial remaining subjects to be addressed by providers of computer-assisted software tools. They should have been first.

The cost of using any of the preceding automated facilities is very high, and various software vendors may specialize in only a few of them. Some vendors are intent on building a fully integrated tool kit. Others will affiliate.

Prior to employing any software tools, knowledge and information standards are clearly needed. CASE tools do not ensure relational thinking. Tools themselves are only as good as the knowledge workers and standards employed to use them.

The cost of knowledge worker training and control can easily dwarf the cost of CASE power tools. However, when an enterprise decides to address knowledge/information management, it will *not* want to embark without automated tool support. The first project in the application of power tools is to identify the global business system that currently exists.

SUMMARY

Finally, it should be clear that business knowledge architecture is a highly disciplined archetype by which to organize, integrate, and manage business knowledge and its information for the entire enterprise.

All business subjects need to be integrated in order to understand how they can be made to interact in order to improve performance, productivity, and profits.

The integrated associations are made possible using standardized subject names and their abbreviated construction sequences to join subjects and display relationships in a consistent way.

BKA is information driven and profit oriented. The background framework of BKA is the profit measurement platform. BKA is the antithesis of the conventional business application orientation. Conversely, BKA follows the principle of 1. No duplicate names or synonyms are allowed. The BKA "semantics umbrella" is a key factor in preventing costly duplications of data, functions, and rules between departments.

BKA provides a linkage between company strategy and its linguistic culture and its environment by relating *internal* source organizations to *external* target resources. BKA is a holistic perspective that allows it to be a galvanizing information force for every manager and supervisor in an enterprise.

The industrial revolution (age) achieved high productivity by fragmenting work as a series of specialized tasks (or an assembly line) for labor and machine functions.

Conversely, the knowledge revolution (age) cannot achieve productivity using isolated pieces of specialized knowlege. Knowledge productivity is only achieved when subject relationships can be quickly accessed together (in parallel) from a global platform using an object-oriented context.

The decompartmentalization of marketing, finance, purchasing, manufacturing, and information management facilitates the symbiotic efforts of the global organizations when departments can easily share information. Every knowledge worker must be able to see the relationship of his or her work to the total business from his or her own work stations. The reason for the current myopia is that the holistic paradigm of business knowledge and its information is not available for all business operatives to observe. A common tool for group productivity must be created.

Therefore, the most important single project of any business is to build its business knowledge infrastructure (tool) for use by all stakeholders.

Figure 6.4 displays the direct relationships which can exist between business subject-term types and business work, rule, and information types when BKA naming standards exist. Figure 6.5 is the master menu for (BKA*) a software tool designed to facilitate knowledge organization and access.

> The source of power and productivity is not money in the hands of a few, but rather knowledge in the hands of many.

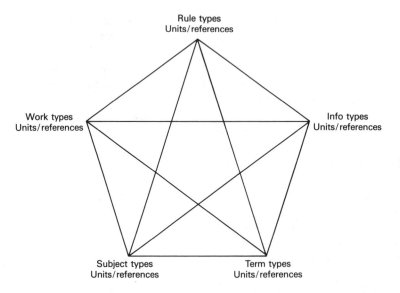

FIGURE 6.4   BKA* integration infrastructure. A synaptic junction of subject abbreviations creates neural pathways between business work, rules, and information.

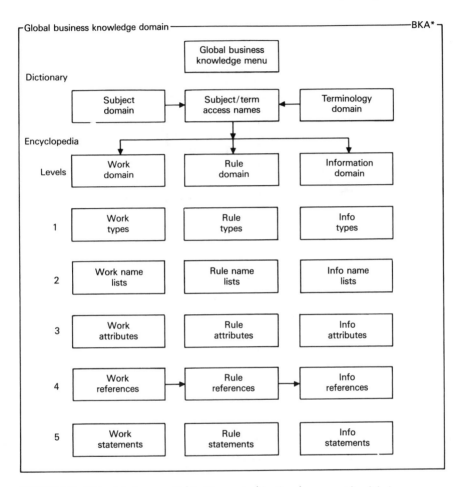

FIGURE 6.5 BKA global menu. Subject/term combination keys provide global search arguments for access to work, rule, and information units.

Chapter 7

Network Architecture

INTRODUCTION

Today it is no longer possible to manage a substantial business efficiently without the use of telecommunications, computers, and networks.

Previous chapters have addressed building architected information, business processes, computer functions, and rules without regard to their physical locations. In many businesses, sales, manufacturing, purchasing, distribution, warehousing, or accounting activities are located at different physical sites. This functional diversity introduces the need for information transfer.

When the physical and logistical information transfer problems are coupled with the previously described data duplications, it is a wonder that business works as well as it does. Total costs of information networks are increasing at an increasing rate. This is due not so much to communication technology costs but rather to the unstructured way communication networks are allowed to expand.

The growth of communication networks has paralleled the piecemeal approach of computerized business applications. Bridges abound using incompatible site-to-site communication hardware and software protocols. The human talent to control them is increasingly dispersed. A proliferation of vendors, protocols, rate changes, transmission speeds, and technical devices has created yet another specialist area to handle the complexity of getting information from one place to another.

The technical community has presented many solutions to the processing, storing, and transfer of data from one work place to another. Video/data terminals, printers, and real-time computer-to-computer communications have given businesses many diverse application options in marketing, production, and product services, but not as an integrated solution (the big prize).

Unfortunately, the same data access problem which exists within information architecture also exists in communication networks. Communication software types abound. Vendors typically establish their own transmission standards and leave the selection of information content to the business user. Organizations repeatedly install disjointed data networks that are made obsolete by new technology, standard changes, cost decreases, or simply data volume that cannot be accommodated.

A premise of this chapter is that a common network architecture is required to define and measure operational tasks and to control information by location. A logistical platform is needed *prior to* the selection of physical networks or communication devices, which, in fact, may not even be required.

This chapter is intent on establishing a perspective for information logistics independent of the fast-changing hardware technology and network software. *What, where, why,* and *how fast* decisions about transmitting information must precede the *how to* transmit. These decisions can affect millions of business outlays yet to come.

The changes to business communication networks can no longer be based solely on technological innovation. The human cost of implementing technical network changes is too large. It is not just a matter of substituting communications hardware and software; the costs of retraining staff are exorbitant. Any change in data communications must be evaluated by the *added value* that remote functional support or remote information usage can earn.

Management must ensure that data communication functions truly produce incremental contributions to profit. As with the previously described business functions, the optimization of only a single part of the global information network will not necessarily improve business profits overall. Business information logistics must primarily address the functional need at the remote site. For control purposes, network information must be integrated with the work, rule, and computer software architectures previously described in order to allow people to work together to maximize wealth.

A metaphor for the interaction and control of remote group work and information support is the subject of this chapter.

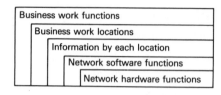

| Business work functions |
| Business work locations |
| Information by each location |
| Network software functions |
| Network hardware functions |

FIGURE 7.1   Network component relationships.

BUSINESS NETWORK COMPONENTS

Before a network can be managed, its major components must be identified and related. Three BKA management tiers are used to establish a framework for the measurement, control, and analysis of network components and their relationships:

1. Work control
2. Information control
3. Network control

A view of network component relationships is depicted in Figure 7.1.

It is appropriate to discuss the decisions that managers must face in controlling their networks.

BUSINESS WORK CONTROL

In Chapter 5, a distinction is drawn among types of work:

1. Business activities (mental work)
2. Business functions (physical work)
3. Machine functions (computer work)

The distinction is important when analyzing work assignments for employees and managers in the network.

The advent of computer and network technology has seemingly reduced the number of, the cost of, and the need for middle-management tiers. The combination has replaced traditional information dispersion functions. However, the need for managers to coordinate the work of people has not been eliminated. If fact, the need has been increased. The technology to simply move more messages, voices, data, and graphical images across networks at faster speeds may have increased effectiveness of the business *function,* but it has not necessarily improved the productivity of the coordination *activity.*

From a global business view, the technical advance of the network is producing a social phenomenon that is gradually affecting employee and management behavior at all levels and locations of the business organization.

Simultaneously with the technological impact, the modern corporation is taking on a new profile or fragmentation. Shareholder sovereignty (control) may be the last hurrah of nineteenth-century capitalism. Institutional investors wag the short-term "immediate profit" behavior of management. Leveraged buy-out psychology preoccupies senior management. Correspondingly, manager sovereignty (control) may be the last hurrah of nineteenth-century business control.

The social pressure from the employee for more ownership, work stability, personal care benefits, and independence from control is causing managers concern about who is productive at the remote sites of the very large corporations.

The arguments of centralization vs. decentralization about *where* business work can best be accomplished to maximize service and minimize costs have largely become irrelevant. The advent of the network has enabled employee (knowledge work) activities and (physical work) functions to be implemented anywhere. Information is brought to the work wherever it is located. Consequently, the primary consideration of network architecture is not a technical one but rather has become a management struggle for political turf. Who will control *where* work is to take place, and who will allow *who* to create, access, and update information? Who will know what is happening is a power issue. Information equals power.

In too many companies, this political dilemma takes the form of computer and hardware acquisition. The power concept of data possession conflicts with the hardware/software economics of the 1990s. Already the initial impact of the stand-alone personal computer (PC) and its private information has given way to the insistence by managers for more global shared public information between sites and departments.

The growth of (wide area and local area) network technology supports the demand for information dispersion. Despite all of the technical mumbo jumbo and interim networking solutions, the primary issue remains: What functional facilities and information are needed to support company work at its work sites? If a strategic integration of information from/to many sites in real time were not needed, the network dilemma would not exist.

> Ten thousand microcomputers, each with nonuniformly structured information, are no substitute for a single integrated information base.

Information is often dispersed so widely or coded so tightly that access is impossible. The usual method of handling the situation is to show the flag of a quick implementation of some spur from what is readily available—new grillwork, new fenders, and new uniforms, but not research to build a better vehicle.

Quickie local systems add to complexity and require more people maintenance at the spur sites. Instead of moving to a lower-cost, integrated, long-range communication strategy, the data disintegration process continues. The resulting human confusion costs are not presented to management—only the low cost of a single personal computer here and there.

Many remote-site managers are spending more time with the intricacies of their DOS to OS personal computer conversions than with customers, products, vendors, and employees.

To control work, the computer master functions (Chapter 5) can be utilized to analyze what work exists and where it can most economically be performed. Box 7.1 displays the master functions which must be considered for remote site implemention.

BOX 7.1

Computer Master Functions

1. Transaction control/recording/switching/transmission
2. Edit/validate
3. File management/create/delete
4. Posting/updating
5. Processing
6. File dating/control
7. Information display/printing

The purpose of the functional classifications is to identify and control computer functions without reference to any specific computer, communication network, hardware, or software.

The generic view (Figure 7.2) displays location options for computer and work functions. If a business transaction (capture and control) were the only remote computer function and all other functions were executed centrally, the information flow would appear as in Figure 7.2.

The display shows the incremental buildup of functions needed as remote sites add their own full-scale computer facility. The off-loading of central host computer functions carries more costs than that of only the remote terminal or microcomputer. Even then, the central computer must still retain all of the same functions to put remote data back together in an integrated and architected way.

Figure 7.2 is not unfamiliar to computer professionals. Managers may not have had the opportunity to reflect on the incremental computer

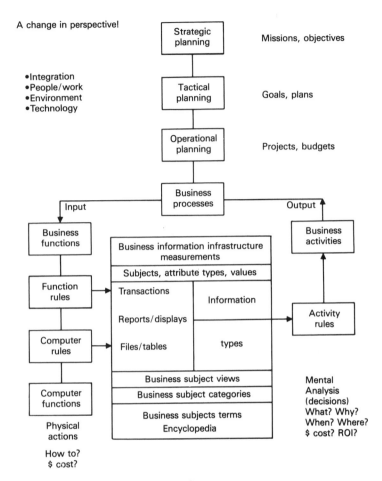

FIGURE 7.2 Information systems architecture.

function and cost buildups that occur when remote sites take on major computer functions.

Too frequently, the rush to decentralize business management seems to imply that the computer facility must also be decentralized. This is not the case where the information base is well architected. Even if functional fragmentation is a political decision, a global architecture is still needed to display, control, and document what work and computer functions exist by location.

There are economic arguments for dispersing computer functions to remote sites. Consider, for example,

1. Transaction (VDT screen) controls
2. Edit/validations (transaction data)
3. Information displays (queries)

All of these functions can require many unique program housekeeping modules, resulting in a large combined load on a central computer. Dispersing these housekeeping functions can free up a great deal of central computer power.

Conversely, other computer functions are more related and can be more economically executed and controlled with the prinicple of 1 at a single location/site:

1. File management
2. File dating
3. Posting/updating
4. Processing/manipulation

(Technical development and programming are centralized activities.)

The relational integrity of the data is easily corrupted in the distributed environment without an enforcement of architectural standards.

Remote work and computer functions are the first manager decisions to be made as a business builds its network. All of the work, rule, and information types identified in Chapter 6 must be assigned and related to each remote site of the enterprise.

BUSINESS INFORMATION CONTROL

Information disintegration and dispersion are a most critical logistical issue. When files are dispersed, data is frequently named incoherently and put in different formats that then require more translations and more conversions. Costly interfaces are then required just to get information together. File control with dispersed data is very costly and difficult to maintain. The information time period problem is a challenge in itself.

Last, architecting the related components of information is complicated by its remote collection of information in various states of semiprocessing.

Many companies handle a single transaction (or piece of data) many times remotely and then again centrally. This excess cost in computer usage, interim people, and machine control goes on because senior managers do not see these excessive costs. They may be led to believe "it's a technical limitation." Some data processing managers see the duplication in many cases but are too buried in the problems of the day to eliminate the duplication.

The term *interface* is the epitome of repetition. It is the failure to do a complete job (when the transaction is initially in hand) that creates higher costs and control problems. The principle of 1 becomes the principle of *too many*.

When the transaction is not brought in from the remote site and validated and processed in its *entirety* in real time, more intermediate layers of middle management are required to analyze control reports and to reenter adjustments. These intermediate sequential methods probably are a continuation of antiquated accounting practices that required a book of original entry followed by subledger and journal posting and then subsequent posting to a general ledger.

The computer, as the chief bookkeeper, is in fact able to update all ledgers (records) *simultaneously* in microseconds or back out transactions just as fast. However, old sequential accounting habits are hard to break. Parallel processing will ultimately prevail. The more computer functions that are distributed remotely, the more auditors will be required to monitor them.

Some technicians claim it takes too much time to update or post multiple file arrays simultaneously and directly. Yet, in the next breath, they are willing to spend hours sorting, controlling, processing batches sequentially, extracting reports in different sequences, reorganizing files, and down-loading whole files to remote PC locations. Some managers are too far removed to note the difference or perceive what the internal speeds of new computers are capable of providing.

Parallel processing to multiple file tables is now possible. The principle of 1 trigger is the future even when multiple remote sites are involved.

Multitiered hardware architecture (micro-mini-host) has proven a disaster for both control and cost. Multivendor hardware and communications protocols further complicate the total problem by requiring more staff to control the transactions and migrations required by dissimilar hardware types.

Management must ensure that

1. All related information files are updated simultaneously for the same time period as soon as data is available
2. The hardware and software used are compatible throughout their company

Many of the most respected experts in the computer industry are touting the emergence of the microcomputer and the flexibility to download files to remote sites. In the next instance, they proclaim the need to integrate information. It is clear that all business departmental processes contribute information to central files and that a large percentage of departments must access the information of other departments.

The up-loads and down-loads of fragmented information can bankrupt most companies. The number of people needed to control fragmented data communication and its maintenance simply do not exist in the market. Clustering 100 independent microcomputers over data lines to retrieve integrated information from separated files adds to cost and wastes time.

Why are fragmented technological solutions implemented? Information infrastructure and control have not been created or managed to prevent this logistical fragmentation. In addition to the methodology gap, there is a management perception and skill gap. Most companies have not prepared for complex remote or central computer integration.

Many companies have trouble getting one computer to work. Networking many computers without common data is ludicrous.

The technology argument persists. If it exists, use it! If it can be done, do it! If you can get it installed, someone will use it for something! Get version 1 on the market, and it can be debugged in 200 subsequent releases! Hardware and software logistical diversity is considered by some companies as the leading edge, but the cost in human talent and subsequent movement into the communication spaghetti bowl proves fatal in the long run.

Frequently, information has been physically described as relational frameworks. However, many companies are still locked into static data bases at many remote sites. For those fortunate enough to utilize relational data bases, their remote information can be indexed and accessed from the computer the way people logically view information without regard to location.

Some computer vendors do not address the problem of information standards and relationships relative to remote locations. They argue that distributed files and data bases can simply continue to use communications lines to join various segments of the existing mess. Keeping them all indexed and synchronized is not the vendor problem.

Controlling the location of all of the human and computer functions is much like the previously discussed consulting ventures. Major projects are continuously needed just to find out what exists. If undocumented changes take place at various sites, only the computer and three programmer artists really know what information is transferred or what it means or costs. Then more money can be spent on reverse engineering software to overcome what was initially poor technique.

The paradox is that the more integrated business information and processes need to become (in the interest of productivity), the more control is required. The more dispersed data processing becomes, the harder that same control is to achieve. Control must be exercised over both the information content and where it is used. The information must be related to its locations.

BUSINESS NETWORK CONTROL

For network control to be achieved, a control architecture is needed. Figure 7.3 is an example of the functional control view that management can address when information, hardware, and software issues are analyzed.

- What type of remote terminal capability is required?
- What types of logic are required at the remote sites?
- What information limitations should exist remotely? On reference files only? On full content files?
- What computer functions are to be performed? Centrally? Remotely?

The answers to these questions should be placed in a simplified network similar to that shown in Figure 7.3. Almost every remote business function will ultimately generate transactions. These transactions require functions to

1. Record and control the transaction itself
2. Edit/validate the transaction

FIGURE 7.3 BKA network architecture (function distribution).

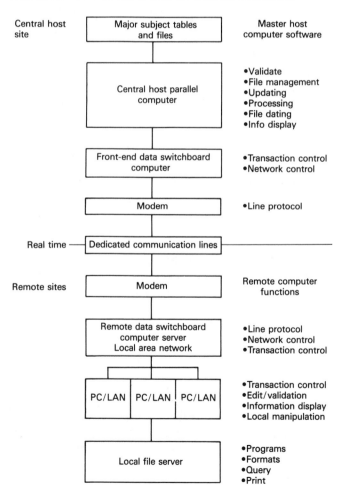

Centralized business functions will be required to

1. Update the files using transactions
2. Manipulate data in the files
3. Control file dating/security
4. Display file information
5. Manage, create/delete existing file types

Computer professionals frequently fail to manage the preceding as a resource. The management of data is the issue when remote-site computerization takes place.

The most important economic factors in transaction handling hinge on

1. The volume of transactions
2. The complexity of the transactions
3. The variety of subfunction processing that the transaction triggers

It is therefore important to name and categorize every type of transaction and relate it to its remote site.

> **Note:** A single report request (information display) can pull some very large computers to their knees. If the information is really not needed, the situations can become ludicrous. The question is why is all of this happening. The answer is the policy of "give users whatever they ask for." In many companies, information control does not take place. Who performs this activity? The answer is, frequently, "no one."

It is common for the enterprise to push computer professionals to respond to immediate requests and forget the ultimate costs of dispersing computer files and functions. They are not paying the bills. They should be controlling the least cost of service.

From Figure 7.3, note that the initial planning should make the assumption that if two or more sites need access to common information, then that information should be consolidated in a central location. Many sites may furnish data to construct that common information base. If the common information is not in one related set of files, then

1. Multiple functions are required to retrieve data using communication lines and mixed access protocols
2. Multiple functions to assemble and format the retrieved data are required

If the common information is in separated files, it cannot be retrieved easily without the logical relational views described in Chapters 4 and 5.

A paradox is established when neither of the two extremes of information processing or storage is selected:

1. All processing central
2. All processing remote

This author submits that access speed, file content availability, and the best economics can be achieved when the computer functions are arrayed as in Figure 7.3.

By placing transaction control and edit/validate computer functions on local computers, the central computer is relieved of as much as 30 percent of its total transaction processing. Then only selective reference data must be transmitted from the central computer to its remote sites.

When dynamic subject content or value information is needed such as inventory prices/quantity or customer/credit data, the local request can communicate directly through the central files. This strategy allows for optimal file content consolidations and central management.

Only reference data is retained locally. For transaction speed and efficiency, data is kept centrally for relational completeness. Only if data content is changed should it be returned to the central depository.

Regardless of where a company elects to perform its master computer functions, a uniform standard architectural view is required to keep it all organized.

When new technologies or business activity requirements are planned, the relational impacts of change must be measured and exposed by viewing functional modules that already exist in a standard format.

Each remote function has a cost. When a remote function is added, the total cost becomes the multiple of the number of sites that implement it. The technological economics of terminal costs, data communication lines, computer operations, and file costs can change; however, the basic functions of the computer will remain relatively static.

Therefore, the basic business and computer functions are major elements in planning central and remote-site facilities. Functions must be named to reference where they are performed, just as information must be named to reflect where business events occur.

Management must
> control remote information functions and costs or submit to an inevitable uncontrolled remote function expansion.

Even when the information and systems architectures are in place and the logistics network is functionally correct, the operations management is the backbone of continuity. If the payroll is not out on time or the inventories are in error by 10 percent, you can forget about strategies, tactics, and planning to look for another job. It does not matter that a third-shift operator or junior programmer did the number on management: The responsibility is at the top to ensure that all of the needed controls and tests are in place and that backup insurance exists.

As whole company strategies and logistics approach 100 percent computer-based control, the line executives cannot allow the nail to be lost. The insurance required in semiautomated systems (in which many interim hands were involved) was considerably less than that required for the fully computerized real-time plants of the future. When the bulldozer is operating at capacity, the earth is moving. When a part breaks, everything stops in the integrated world of data and computer functions. This time the original programmers are not available. If they were, they couldn't learn the alternative steps fast enough to restart a manual operation.

The danger of work stoppage exists when labor-intensive work shifts to full automation and only its benefits are perceived. The new problems of automation and their checkpoints are only beginning to be understood. The computer itself is the only facility that has the capability and is fast enough to recoup its own failure or that of a humanly induced logic error or virus.

Business functions at remote sites emit business transactions every second of the day. The trend is clearly from a sequential operation to a simultaneous environment; with the latter thousands of dissimilar transactions can arrive at the computer in random order in real time. They can be selected and processed immediately.

Some companies record transactions, summarize them daily, and send them to another location for more processing, fragmentation, and summarization. Each step requires checkpoint costs. The same scenario exists for reports that are produced. The reports are reviewed, and more adjustments create more reports for middle-management to correct. The cycle goes on.

Network control should incorporate its own measurements of the following:

The percent of time in-process work is lost in idle time
The percent of time work is in a position to be started
The percent of time equipment is idle due to underutilization
The percent of time the network fails

If information is not displayed on the network when the preceding productivity gaps occur, the operational work flow can become one time-gap nightmare of change after another. The stress on people is unbelievable because one change begets another before the first is resolved. People productivity under these conditions adds to a self-perception crisis that is responsible for even less productivity. A shift in managment perspective is required from knee-jerk reaction to a steady flow of continuous work.

The lack of information, systems, and network architecture standards in a more fully automated work environment is responsible for the waste of automated resources. Many industries are automating and reautomating but are still losing ground because their automation and networking is piecemeal and not integrated in its implementation.

Real-time networks can provide a global facility for all sites of the business to access uniform up-to-date data regardless of location.

The transition from sequential processes to simultaneous parallel processes did not alert companies to the absolute need for network architecture. Traditionally managements clung to four premises:

1. The central computer host was not powerful enough to control all transactions of the business simultaneously.
2. The data was not important enough to be updated and processed on a same-day basis.
3. Communication lines were too costly/unreliable to support real-time recording from remote sites.
4. Transaction detail could be handled more economically in batch mode.

Smart managements have discovered that all of these premises have given way to the speed and cost of new technology, parallel process computers, faster and more reliable software, lower-cost file storage and communication lines, and the advantage of up-to-date information. New applications and volume increases have led to an increase in total data communication outlays.

As various types of transactions register with the computer, it must be fast enough to control, edit, validate, update, and manipulate the values of each transaction to every section of the total set of file array and to reflect the immediate new status for all points in the network before the next incoming transaction.

The principle of 1 must exhaust each transaction in its entirety so that no subsequent batch processing or interfaces are required. What this amounts to is a general ledger that is up-to-date by the second, complete with all historical accumulations.

To accomplish and control the principle, transaction modularity is an absolute requirement. Integrated relational file control with direct file addressing for data elements will require a highly regulated information architecture.

Those companies that have their information architecture and associated computer function mapping together will be able to take advantage of the new superfast, low-cost parallel computer switchboard technology of the future.

The net result of simultaneity is that no work function station (local or remote) will wait for another in order to continue its work. Work gaps will close and minimize costs.

The concept of up-to-date (just-in-time) is strategically important enough to merit a couple of examples to show its added strategic value.

It is no secret that some airline computer reservation systems have become added-value assets without which the company could not profit.

The marketing and sales support function includes the following:

1. The customer or travel agent accesses a computer from a remote site.
2. Flights, route options, facilities, and costs are displayed on terminals, and selections are entered.
3. A customer credit card is validated and authorized.
4. A price is computed including other airline connections.
5. A seat/flight number is assigned.
6. The seat inventory by flight is decremented.
7. The ticket is printed.
8. Interconnecting airlines are booked/credited.
9. Funds are transferred from the credit source.

All of the business functions are performed almost simultaneously from many remote sites. Most data processing operations are not yet this integrated because the information, system, and logistical architecture does not exist. Consequently, many businesses are unable to meet the competition, achieve the added value, or meet the customer service level.

If data processing and information support is not integrated, then one function must wait for the next, sometimes for days. These delays incur excess costs because people functions are injected between computer functions. If the principle of simultaneity were not employed by airlines for reservations and seat inventories, the number of customer callbacks would be prohibitive, and productivity would crash.

The purpose in reviewing the example is to alert managers to invest in network architecture to plan long-range strategic information with remote-site support functions.

The number of subjects and functions are too great to allow any more systems to be designed on napkins without the global view of the total company impact. While batch processing may get basic business jobs done and produce after-the-fact reports, future competition demands that managements be able to link their systems on line to the customers, vendors, and outside entities they serve or are served by. Standard user interfaces are essential to this effort.

The business processes, transactions, computer functions, communications, and information architectures must be planned together, not one piece at a time. Remote sites must be globally networked in real time with the central host site. Local control of networks is the hard way to get the integrated job done.

SUMMARY

In summary, Figure 7.2 depicts some of the functional decisions that must be made when multiple remote sites exist. The physical placement of the business and computer functions can have a profound effect on overall business costs. Some business functions create a large volume of transactions and require many terminal devices to record business events. Some remote business processes can require access to a wide array of information and access to many information relationships. The distance, time, and response speed factors are the prime determinants of communication facility costs. It is clear that the expansion of remote business and computer functions has a multiplier effect in required automation devices that may initially appear to reduce business costs.

The network support required to operate and control the new technology can dwarf terminal device and transmission costs. Without a careful analysis of the decision factors invoked by Figure 7.3, effective network management may not be achieved.

The real danger in remote processing is found when each remote business unit creates its own exclusive information and rules. Network architecture must be used to keep track of where business functions, computer functions, controls, terminal devices, files, communication devices, and information are physically located.

If the preceding subjects are left as stand-alone islands of automation, it will be impossible to understand how they support each other or how to control them.

The business knowledge program must put it all together. Communication networks need to be controlled by uniform work function types at each location.

> Without knowledge of network integration (work, rules, information, and systems logistics) business operations are severely constrained.

PART THREE

BUSINESS KNOWLEDGE IMPLEMENTATION

Part One describes a perspective regarding the importance of business knowledge and its scope and preservation.

Part Two describes a business knowledge architecture and its parts and relationships for structuring the long-term asset.

Part Three describes how a knowledge resource can be implemented by migration rather than by a whole system replacement.

The movement to knowledge architecture will be relatively fast for a few companies because they are acquiring high-quality information engineers. They are investing the long-term resource dollars necessary to pursue the construction of knowledge standards and contents.

Some companies are totally unaware of what is needed to enhance business performance through computerized knowledge acquisition. They are haphazardly investing in piecemeal computer software packages, technical hardware, and technicians with limited perspectives without an overall view of the global enterprise knowledge platform.

Most experts agree that relational knowledge orientation will be a prime consideration in integrated systems of the future. Many companies are already implementing knowledge-based management and inference problem solving techniques. Computer-stored intelligence is not a quick and easy package installed over a weekend. It requires a specific project and a step-by-step approach and demands that all units of a business construct a uniform knowledge base.

Part Three is directed toward helping those companies that want to embark on a knowledge program but have not been able to define a specific plan for action. Although the *what, why,* and *structures* for the program can be meticulously described, the migration perception is the real challenge. Most businesses already have a large investment in their current systems. Millions of lines of computer code, volumes of procedure manuals and a culture of unwritten business rules govern how the companies conduct their current business.

Quick system replacements are impractical regardless of the number of computer-assisted tools available. Business knowledge architecture is a mind set required to understand and utilize enterprise data.

Defining, relating, or transplanting even a small piece of most business systems is a major investment. The human knowledge contained within most business departments has been accumulated over a long period of time and is continually changing. Restructuring and relating computerized knowledge, information, and rules will require a long-range plan. The migration plan requires a long-range vision of the platform toward which even the smallest project must converge.

Having installed knowledge programs, this author can testify to the many human trials and chaos that a companywide change in perception can invoke.

The statement of Machiavelli may be appropriate in the introduction of knowledge architecture.

"It must be remembered that there is nothing more difficult to plan, more doubtful of success, than the creation of a new idea. For the initiator has the enmity of all who would profit by the preservation of the old institution, and merely lukewarm defenders in those who would gain by the new one."
Niccolo Machiavelli 1469–1527

The knowledge development project must address

- The business organization
- The architectural blueprint
- The migration plan
- The internal company change strategy

Chapter 8

A Business Knowledge Project

INTRODUCTION

It is one thing to extort and structure knowledge and another matter to implement a knowledge management (KM) program.

The purpose of this chapter is to describe what is involved in implementing a business knowledge project. The final product of the KM project will be a work environment, tools, and a knowledge index facility. The tools created will facilitate access to and display of

1. What functions exist
2. What rules exist
3. What information exists
4. How subjects relate
5. How the total system works (model)
6. How modular changes are effected

The product deliverable is an integrated structure that yields knowledge about knowledge. The infrastructure (end product) is a physical view describing how all system components should work together. A foreground image reflects how the current system actually works. When duplications or deficiencies exist, they are prominently displayed with newly structured background formats to be used for migration.

The knowledge architecture is an entity separate from the actual knowledge system contents that it contains. The BKA asset is a mirror image of and describes the working knowledge facility.

The knowledge asset must be *designed* to reflect the global interactivity of its subjects. It must describe how every part of the business interacts on the new platform in terms of those standard elements described in Chapters 4 through 7.

The asset must be computerized for recall because humans cannot remember all of the subjects or how they relate. By using architecture, nomenclature, syntax, semantics, and common tools to explain and standardize knowledge, groups of knowledge workers can cooperate more easily.

Current business knowledge can be defined in terms of new reusable standard parts; knowledge implementation strategy is based on replacing sections of the current system, using those standard parts. Whenever a part of the system requires modification, standard data pieces are used to avoid duplications and to build new modules.

Several phases and tasks are required for the knowledge program to be created. This chapter is a discussion of those phases, activities, and tasks needed for the two-part implementation:

1. Construct an empty framework
2. Migrate to and populate the facility

ORGANIZATIONAL REQUIREMENTS

A major theme of this book is knowledge for profit. It is appropriate to discuss the knowledge development team as the first step in implementing the knowledge program.

If a company has a data processing department, it might seem logical to delegate the management of the project to the data processing staff. It is the opinion of many experts that the data processing department is the last place you would want to entrust the responsibility for a knowledge program. The reason for this opinion is that the implementors must understand business products and processes and how their rules work. The effort is not a data processing project even though the tools of that technology are used.

Participants must have a vested interest in the profits of the business and be charged with and know how to make a dollar by structuring their business knowledge and that of others. This means selecting experienced managers from the mainstream business processes.

As with the selection of any special project group of major consequences, the selection and qualification of people are crucial to success. It doesn't matter if the individual ever wrote a computer program or can spell *infrastructure*. It does matter if that person

1. Has the instinct for profits
2. Has the perception of how knowledge affects profits
3. Has the patience to construct the new asset

If the right temperaments cannot be located, then the effort should not be undertaken.

The personnel of the team should have diverse backgrounds that cover all aspects of the business and its relation to the industry. The team will have experience at the management level in a variety of business process disciplines:

1. Marketing
2. Manufacturing
3. Personnel/training
4. Finance/accounting
5. Distribution/transportation
6. Engineering/research
7. Corporate planning

They will understand that their effort will require a major dedication of time, not the least of which will be learning *how* knowledge and information must be constructed and how it can be used by the entire company. If managers are to reorient the entire company, then, of course, they are the first in line to be reoriented.

Their personality, character, charisma, mental scope, and communication skills have to be excellent. Probably, the first choices would appear to be managers with high intelligence, personal motivation, and achievement quotients. The most important element is that of working as a team for the good of the total company. Parochial areas of responsibility will have to be subordinated for the common good of the total organization. Short tempered, quick-solution, dominant, egocentric characteristics can defeat the purpose of the cooperative venture.

The members of the team will cross into each other's domains. They will define and structure the business rules. No stone of productivity can be left unturned. Those selected are clearly the company leaders of tomorrow. Assembling this combination of skills and personal attributes can easily take a year.

Some managers may perceive this project to be unimportant or a career sidetrack. Nothing could be further from the truth. If any protest too much, they are not the ones up to the challenge. Persistence and patience will clearly be their greatest virtues. Conversely, no one can be looking for early retirement. They must know that careers and incentives are at stake.

Two parameters must be firmly established:

1. The budgets to fund the KM project over a one- to two-year period
2. The recognition and reward for those who work it through to implementation

In projects of this type, some companies can fail to understand the importance of these two ingredients for success. Quality staff selections are needed. If multiple substitutions take place, the project can become a revolving door for terminations and retirements.

Some companies have expected the creation of a business model to be the end in itself. Frequently the business model ends up on the shelf because the organizational culture and the subsequent implementation steps are hazy.

In other companies the evidence is equally clear that permanent knowledge is their most important asset. There is evidence that major companies are in pursuit of the knowledge asset at an increasing rate. Those companies that are most productive in these ventures know how to select the right people as the first priority.

A sample of the knowledge board organization is described by Figure 8.1. They knowledge board must

1. Be in touch with but free of daily operations
2. Be closely tied to the strategic planning of the company
3. Include highly skilled *detail people* who know business operations

Since the team size is relatively small (7 to 10), none of its members can be expected to be distracted from their knowledge board tasks. Figure 8.2 is a sample of the knowledge board's support group, which is needed for the functional documentation work. The mechanics of entering data to a computer, documenting current rules, running reports, and structuring complex rule relationships will be major tasks of the support group.

FIGURE 8.1 Business knowledge board organization.

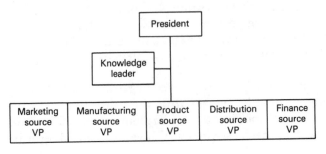

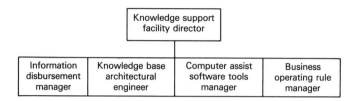

FIGURE 8.2 Business knowledge support organization. The knowledge planning board must operate separately from the system development staff.

So far we have managed to keep the technical community at enough distance to prevent computer technology *how to* from corrupting the *what* and *why* aspects of the project. The knowledge board can be kept well informed with various technology presentations. Their mission is not to decide which computer or robot will implement or update their knowledge. They are concerned with packaging the knowledge to drive computers.

By establishing an independent knowledge board, systems development, computer operations, and technical data base activities can better operate with the assurance they will be furnished company priorities, rules, strategies, and goals. The traditional data processing organization is production oriented. Its perspective is usually short-term products and fire maintenance. Its strength is oriented to *how* things can be done rather than *why* they should be done or *what* should be done.

By developing a global view of the current and future company needs in a common architecture, the knowledge board can direct the right projects to be prioritized and sequenced without the day-to-day political pressure. Data processing staffs have typically supported operational departments separately. They have not been able to support the company in a globally strategic manner.

The knowledge acquired will cut across functional business units. The knowledge engineers will build the information architecture and create the enterprise model, which in turn will embrace business rules. System migration projects must be synchronized in a relational way. Once the information architecture is in place and consistent with the enterprise model, corporate objectives/goals can be supported by knowledge architecture.

The knowledge architecture concept requires a willingness to concentrate an intellectual intensity that does not come easily within some corporate cultures. The knowledge board must change the company from organization and political perceptions to customer service, product quality, and profit perceptions.

In summary, the following organizational activities are needed:

1. Select the knowledge board leader.
2. Select the board members.

3. Select the methodology to accumulate knowledge.
4. Train the board in the architecture.
5. Select software tools to support subject relationships.

The importance of selecting a qualified team cannot be overemphasized.

KNOWLEDGE BOARD TRAINING

Many companies have adopted packaged software techniques using a variety of methodologies. The proper match between the methods to be used and the software support for the knowledge project is a crucial factor.

It is important for the knowledge board to study the available methods and techniques. It is this author's recommendation that the best sources are those companies that have attempted to implement them. Few companies will fail to advise what they would do if they could start over on the KM project.

There are many computer-assisted system engineering (CASE) design aids that almost claim to allow company missions and objectives to be converted directly to computer code and data bases, untouched by human hands. Unfortunately, many of these techniques require

1. An army of specialists
2. A preponderance of nonbusiness terminology
3. Large guru consulting and training contracts
4. More technical middlemen and translators

Some companies have been very successful in creating their own business model, sometimes with the minor assistance of outside consultants. Problems usually arise when the detail follow-on architectures must be extended to lower detail levels or the project teams attempt application projects without global views.

The knowledge team must be thoroughly trained in information architecture techniques so that objectives, goals, business models, computer functions, and information can be expressed as related entitites, as described in previous chapters.

The knowledge planning board will require a metaphor to describe the current system using the new architecture. The knowledge project must be viewed as a long-term migration, not a package installation. It begins by a thorough examination of the current system as its starting point. It is no secret that some techniques have run into some major criticism as being too "big blue sky" that can't be implemented. Notions that architectures, concentrated analysis, and disciplined nomenclature (as described in Chapters 4 through 6) can be avoided by the use of CASE tools are erroneous. In fact, the architecture must drive the CASE tools.

MIGRATION STRATEGY

When senior management decides to implement a knowledge repository, the project must be regarded as a major goal of the company. The principal obstacles to migration will be human, financial, and technical resources.

The business may already have a well-entrenched computerized system and staff in place. The investment in the current system may be substantial, and enhancements may be under way that already use a large part of the current development resources. Since the key business managers are presumably occupied in today's work, it is only natural to ask, "Who has time to work on a knowledge repository?" Yet, the current staff managers are the very people who must be responsible for migrating to the new environment. At first, this would seem to be an impasse.

Business systems analysts and computer programmers work with selected business managers to carve out small pieces of work, implement one piece, and interface the subapplication to an existing business process. Unfortunately, that approach requires many complex interfaces, time sequencing, and an elapsed time period of years to complete. The investment in fragmentation is substantial. While this building approach is criticized, there does not appear to be any better solution. The concept of an integrated migration is frequently discarded in the "heat of battle" to (quick, quick) implement a new disjointed piece.

There are two conflicting frameworks in the migration to a knowledge base:

1. Knowledge structures used by people
2. Program structures used with computers

Planning and architecting knowledge must merge both of the preceding to a single orientation, presented in Chapters 4 and 7. During migration, the perceptions of people are frequently changed if they are asked to first learn a common set of standard expressions before they define their knowledge about business rules, information requirements, and computer programs.

The precise thinking that is invoked by the use of relational standards can unnerve some people who are not inclined to be precise. Some major problems in the business may be uncovered that participants may consider personal failures. Adequate care must be taken with people to avoid personal blame.

Frequently, the exposure of problems creates a defensive environment. If each problem is immediately fixed, one at a time, the real cause surfaces elsewhere. If a total perception can be initially applied, then the business staff can work toward global solutions that address several problems simultaneously.

Few companies can afford to build a new global system or replace thousands of computer code lines. A migration requires a new perspective. Most enterprises "can" afford to architect a global BKA to provide a description of what is required, why it is required, and its effect on the whole.

A migration to a knowledge base environment can be compared to the construction of a new building. The first step is a clear set of plans and standards relating to the purpose, components, and use of the knowledge structure. Standard components of the trade are first identified as to where they can be used to minimize costs. New bolts do not have to be fabricated where standard bolts exist.

A migration to a knowledge base requires all of the plans, blueprints, and parts to be identified as standard components. The key to the migration is to have the majority of information, functions, and logistical architected pieces identified before any assembly is attempted. Integrated construction can begin only when any/all of the pieces can be related using standard connections (very much like a Lego set).

Traditionally, new systems evolve replacing current functions, maintaining some current information, creating new file information, changing business rules, and, in many cases, adapting new hardware, software, and programming languages. The number of simultaneous changes may be more surgery than the computerized company patient can cope with. New appendages, complexity, and costs may kill the patient or result in a mutant.

The secret to an effective migration to a new knowledge and information system is the creation of a standardized structural *shell* to scaffold the current system. The modular shell has the advantage that incremental pieces/costs can be inserted at a graduated pace. The end result is not an ad hoc set of applications joined together randomly.

The scaffold is, in fact, the architectural framework presented in Chapters 4 through 7. The knowledge migration strategy requires that every project converge toward a new integrated knowledge base. If business functions, rules, or information is required from the current system in order to support any project, then each project must include exclusive use of new standard, reusable, and architected components. Each project, therefore, initially must incur a slightly higher cost and longer time period to implement using the new standards.

Gradually, as reusable standard components are created, the incremental system construction costs can be reduced. The traditional temptation might be to continue to append directly to the current system, especially if the enhancements are minor and enough resistance to standard discipline erupts. This ad hoc approach can only delay the total migration and rob scarce resources that otherwise could be dedicated to building a long-range foundation. With an architected approach, there are no minor projects since all contribute to a new global integration.

Business Knowledge Architecture (BKA) is a modular standard that allows managers, business operatives, and computer professionals to use the identical nomenclature, business rules, and blueprints to transform the current system into the new environment while the ship is under way. The same system development outlays, which would normally be applied to patching into the current system, are instead directed toward the metamorphosis of the long-range integrated migration. The goal is not any single business application. The goal is a global infrastructure for storing and expanding knowledge and information for use by the whole company. It is subject relational and modular for ease of understanding and change.

A two-part project implementation concept for a knowledge infrastructure is frequently difficult to visualize. The two distinct projects are mirror images:

1. Knowledge framework projects consist of indexes, structures, and descriptions of work, rules, and information called *metainformation*.
2. Business projects consist of work contents and actual information values inserted into the global framework on a project-by-project basis.

BUSINESS KNOWLEDGE FRAMEWORK PROJECT

The construction of a knowledge scaffold (business knowledge accounts) can be compared to establishing an expansible financial chart of accounts. Five parallel phases help to control the activities of the framework project. These phases involve all levels of the management staff. The scope of the project and its relationships to be identified are shown in Figure 8.3.

Each of the phases in Figure 8.3 will have to be addressed. Clearly, all of the relationships can be initially identified. The long-range standards for the framework can be identified. To display the context of the extended architecture, some contents and values can be inserted into the framework. The majority of the content will be deferred until the actual implementation of values in ongoing business projects.

Phase I involves the senior management staff and the knowledge board previously described. Their activities include the following:

1. Create the mission statements of the project.
2. Create the objective statements for the project.
3. Communicate the knowledge system mission to middle management.
4. Initiate knowledge architecture standards.
5. Train the middle management of the company in the concepts of the company business model and its use: business processes, functions, and rule standards.

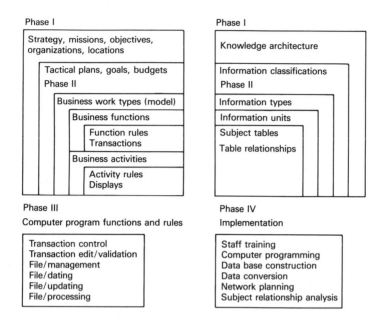

FIGURE 8.3   Business knowledge framework project (implementation phases).

Phase II involves the middle managers and the knowledge board. Their activities include the following:

1. Create the company business model: business processes, functions, and rules.
2. Define the subobjectives and goals of each of the processes.
3. Define the major problems and success factors of each business unit.
4. Define the major business measurement criteria of each process and how they contribute to profits.
5. Identify the problems that are related to and occur between processes.
6. Identify business rules that affect multiple processes.
7. Identify the minimum base information required for each process.

Phase II also involves exclusive knowledge board activities. These activities include the following:

1. Establish the information architecture standards, information categories, subject names, business processes, functions, and activities (Chapters 4 and 5).
2. Select automation facilities to support the selected methodology.
3. Identify all business information types for each business process, function, and activity (transactions, reports, files, tables).
4. Name the entities identified using standard nomenclatures.

Phase III involves the knowledge board and the systems staff. Their activities include the following:

1. Train in the computer master functions/subfunction documentation standards (Chapter 5).
2. Train in the relational automation tool.
3. Document the current business transactions that drive the current computer system using the standard naming conventions.
4. Document each of the computer program functions (CPFs) (transaction control, edit/validate, file management, updating, processing, file dating, information display).
5. Relate all information elements to their corresponding information types.
6. Name and join information elements to their respective computer rules using a relational data base as a tool.

Phase IV involves the review of the first three phases of activities by the combined senior management, middle management, the knowledge board, and information planning staff. Their activities will include the following:

1. Relate the company missions, objectives, and goals to the business processes, functions, and activities.
2. Relate the business processes, functions, and activities to their driving rules.
3. Relate the information required to support the functions and activities.
4. Prioritize the sequence of functions, rules, and information tables to be constructed for the common infrastructure.
5. Create the information menu shell and indexes to control the company knowledge base.

Box 8.1 displays those human perspectives which will be affected in the migration to new architected knowledge and tools.

BOX 8.1

Knowledge Migration Perspective Shift	
FROM	TO
Unique system designs for each business application	A common data nucleus design and information architecture utilized by all processes
Unique information report formats	Standard information reporting structures
Files dedicated to specific business applications	Integrated data bases common to all business work
Batch processing	Real time query/updating
Departmental services	Total company services

FROM	TO
Software tools for technicians	Software tools for business operatives
Applications dependent on vendor hardware, databases, software	Applications independent vendor hardware, databases, software
Unique program application rules	Reusable program modules, building blocks
System flow diagram views	Encapsulated object views
Phased system development	"Lego set" expansion development
Programmer directed file access	Business operative element access
File access based on record references	Direct data element access based on relational symbolic word string calculated addresses
Sequential application file updates	Multiple parallel file updates

It is appropriate to reiterate that the business knowledge implementation involves a major global project followed by many subprojects. The first of the four milestones below apply to the global project.

FIVE MAJOR MILESTONES OF MIGRATION TOWARD A GLOBAL KNOWLEDGE SYSTEM

1. Create a global relational business information architecture.
2. Construct an architected relational business work model of all business functions.
3. Implement all current *file management* through the use of relational subject base tables.
4. Extract all new *information displays* using relational subject tables.
5. Implement all new systems projects using only the new information base and current business work rules where needed.

BUSINESS PROJECT IMPLEMENTATIONS

The implementation phase of the knowledge project is an iterative process and builds on the base framework previously constructed. Initially, the knowledge base is only a reflection of what the current system is and what it does. As projects evolve, managers of each process are responsible for updating the functions, rules, and information units that populate the global structure. Figure 8.4 depicts the phases of the global business project in which the global knowledge framework is to be created.

The current physical system may be completely different from the relational view of the architecture. The knowledge board is responsible for keeping track of all of the information categories of, relationships of, and proposed changes to the existing system.

The system development expenditures used to plan and organize the global "bookkeeping" for the company knowledge system will be miniscule compared to any *no-control* alternative. Preconceived notions of software package and computer hardware panaceas are dramatically altered when the business model is exposed as a unified global perspective.

FIGURE 8.4 BKA global project phases.

<u>Phase 1</u> Project requirements (PRJ__REQ)

Select information units
from information domain types.
Create new info units required
using naming standards
and relational tables.

Information architecture

```
Relational data base
  Categories
  Types
  Subjects
  Subject attributes
  Subject references
  Subject statements
```

<u>Phase 2</u> Project analysis (PRJ__ANL)

Select work units
from work domain types.
Create new work units required
using function naming and
construction standards.

Systems Architecture

<u>Phase 3</u> Project design (PRJ__DSG)

Create tables for file
management (FM) functions.

Use relational tables of
new information architecture
to control the current system.

Insert transaction contects
into new relational data base
tables as required.

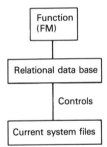

<u>Phase 4</u> Project programming (PRJ__PRG)

Extract all information using
new relational tables.

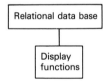

<u>Phase 5</u> Project implementation (PRJ__IPL)
for each sub project

Implement all new projects using
new relational tables.

Use new functional modules
to replace current logic or
add new logic.

NOTE: Since all of the current
elemental data is converted into
the relational base in phase 4,
it is available for use by all
new functional modules.

Relational data base

```
Function 1    VVVVVVV
              VVVVVVV
Function 2    VVVVVVV
              VVVVVVV
Function 3    VVVVVVV
              VVVVVVV
```

V = values

The migration to the global information program cannot be viewed by companies as an immediate replacement of all procedures, computer programs, and hardware that exist. Many companies that have attemped overnight total conversions have been brought to their knees. There are simply too many tasks to perform. A key migration strategy is to define all current subsystems in new architectural formats. In this way it will become clear

1. What does not exist in the current system
2. What should exist in the new information system
3. Where current changes affect the global system

It is usually a tedious task to define the existing system. Frequently, business operatives do not know what the current system is or what rules exist. It is always easier to prescribe new rules without regard for the *new problems* that new rules can create. It is human nature to prescribe how a function should be performed rather than to explain why it should be performed at all. Under the BKA migration technique, every system project must be initialized and defined with reference to the existing global system using the standards of the new architecture. Figure 8.5 is a global check list of related categories which each project phase must identify in order to ensure completeness when implementing systems changes.

The target base for the longterm migration begins with a globally architected relational knowledge facility of the existing system. The physical facility itself is very much like a large empty relational matrix of tables into which data from the current system will be inserted over time on a project-by-project basis. In the early stages of implementation, some information can simply be copied into the new integrated data base structure. All projects will eventually converge to the global framework.

In a series of subsequent steps, remaining data can be intercepted at their *point of earliest availability* and patched directly into the new structure while the old data plant is still operating. At this point, dual data base technologies will exist side by side (i.e., IMS/IDMS, DB2/ORACLE, etc.).

After these initial patching steps are completed, some standard modules for the basic business transactions and functions must be coded modularly as subfunctions.

It is important to draw the distinction between creating the global framework for identification of what currently exists and the actual substitution of newly architected computer code for that currently in use or as new requirements. Actual recoding can be delayed until each subproject is identified as ready to implement within the global structure.

One of the major errors to be avoided in implementation is any attempt to change business rules and computer rules during the migration to the new architecture. Report, file, and rule changes are frequently introduced, and too much change takes place concurrently. Computer

Standard business domains and entities			BKA* life cycle phases			
			PRJ REQ −I−	PRJ ANL −II−	PRJ DSG −III−	PRJ PRG −IV−
> Work domain (hierarchy) − − − − − − − − − − − − − −(Context)		−−				
|.X Business missions (Business)	MIS	x				
|> X Business objectives (Business)	OBJ	x				
|.> X Business goals/problems (Business)	GOL	x				
|..> X Business projects (Business)	PRJ	x				
|...> X Business processes (Business)	PRC	x				
|....> X Business activities (Employee)	ACT	x	x		x	
|.....> X Business functions (Employee)	FNC	x	x		x	
|........X Business jobs (Employee)	TSK	x	x		x	
|.........X Business tasks (Employee)	JOB	x	x		x	
|...>......X Computer jobs (Computer)	CJB		x	x	x	
|..........>X Computer programs (Computer)	PRG		x	x	x	
|..........>X Computer program functions (Computer)	CPF		x	x	x	
> − − − − − −> Rule domain (hierarchy) − − − − − − −						
|........>......X Measurement (Rules)	MRT	x	x	x	x	
|........>...>X Organization (Rules)	ORT	x	x	x	x	
|........>....>>X Location (Rules)	LRT	x	x	x	x	
|........>...>>>X Resource (Rules)	RRT	x	x	x	x	
|........>..>>>>X Transaction (documents) (Rules)	TRT	x	x	x	x	
|........>..>>>>>X Product (Rules)	PRT	x	x	x	x	
> − − − − − −> − − − −> Information domain (hierarchy) − − − − − −						
|...........>>>>>>X Data bases (Computer)	DBT		x	x		
|...........>>>>>.X Data segments (Computer)	DBS		x	x		
|...........>>>>>..X Files (records) (Computer)	FIL		x	x		
|........>..>>>>>.>X Tables (Computer)	TBL			x		
|........>..>>>>>....X Displays (Computer)	DST	x	x	x	x	
|........>..>>>>>.....X Reports (Computer)	RPT	x	x	x	x	
|........>..>>>>>......X Transactions (Computer)	TRS		x	x	x	
|− − − − − − − − − − − −> Data domain (global) − − − − − − −						
|........>>>>>>.>>>>>X Elements (Data)	ELE	x	x	x	x	
|............................>X Subjects (Business)	SBJ	x				
|.............................>X Terms (Business)	TRM	x				

FIGURE 8.5   BKA project component relationships, project life cycle components, and phases, business project productivity performance measurements to be identified: (1) counts of all existing entities, (2) $ value of all existing entities, (3) counts of all entity changes, (4) $ value of all entity changes, (5) counts of all entity errors, (6) $ value of all entity errors.

code is frequently not debugged, and the comparison of old and new data values becomes too complex for business operatives to absorb. There are too many simultaneous changes that can create chaos.

It may seem ludicrous to suggest that old logic be utilized in the initial modules of migration. However, the migration strategy serves itself well in setting the complete modular architecture in place prior to new projects and rules. This 1:1 approach also trains the technical staff in fast modular replacement techniques. Traditionally, it has been too easy to condemn the current system and charge off into new logic only to discover that 90 percent of the old logic had to be retained or that one change created the need for many other changes.

A functional modular approach of an architected migration has the advantage of lowering new system development costs and providing current and new information immediately to business managers. The two-stage migration does not yield applications per se such as payables, receivables, inventory, or order packages. The new information facility is created, and all *applications* of the business are controlled through a common array of work, rule, and information command modules and relational tables.

When the global migration to the new architecture is well along, management can begin to specify what modules are to be prioritized as new projects. In some cases, new reports alone will be adequate to support business activities. In other cases, new calculations, rules, and data may be needed for better information results. In still other cases, new work support functions may be needed to edit, validate, network, and control the accumulation of new data.

The preceding migration strategy demands a shift from the traditional one-time systems conversion perception to a long-range migration concept. Some associated deliverables are listed as tables in Box 8.2.

BUSINESS STAFF TRAINING

The implementation of the knowledge system will require a shift in the perspective of many business operatives. Staff training must be initiated in a variety of subject areas:

- Information nomenclature
- Business models and process architecture
- Information architecture
- Computer system architecture
- Logistical architecture
- Data dictionary and planning library tools
- Business decision rule identification
- Modular computer program construction
- Communication and network architectures

Management will have to ensure that these subjects are presented to all levels of company management and that future information processing budgets address the specific use of these disciplines. The information program and its disciplines are not the exclusive purview of a single department.

A major advantage of this disciplined training is that it has immediate payback to the productivity of the company:

1. Business operatives begin to learn and appreciate their jobs in a more structured way with a productivity perspective.
2. Communications between interacting departments improve as each business operative can see the measurements and problems of other departments affected by their performance.

BOX 8.2

Business Encyclopedia Tables (Sample)

CATEGORY	CONTENT
Business measurements	Business measurement units
Company accounts	Account names, numbers
Company organizations	Organization names, numbers
External business units	Business unit names
Company locations	Physical location names, numbers
Business objectives/goals	Objective/goal statements
Business strategies	Strategy indexes, statements
Business processes	Process names, numbers
Business functions	Function names, numbers
Business tasks	Task numbers, names, measurements
Business transactions	Transaction names, numbers
Business rules	Rule names, numbers
Computer systems	System names, numbers
Information architecture	Information categories, data levels, data classes, names, numbers
Environmental units	Data names
Status units	Data names
Time period units	Data names
Units of measure	Data names
Computer files	File names, numbers
Data elements	Element names, numbers
Computer programs	Program names, numbers
Reports	Report names, numbers
Computer VDT screens	VDT screens, numbers
Business function changes	Function numbers
System projects	Project names, numbers, statements
Customers	Customer names, numbers
Products	Product names, numbers, prices, costs
Vendors	Vendor names, numbers
Carriers	Vendor names, numbers
Employees	Employee names, numbers

---

3. New and more productive ideas are formulated by managers when they are given a structured way to express more productive ways to improve the total business. Knowledge is captured and preserved.

4. Business managers are in a much better position to state the need for storing their knowledge and information.

The training program should be administered by the knowledge board organization with the support of the human resource department. Once the training program has been formulated, a priority segment of one of the mainstream business processes should be selected to test the training adequacy. This training should encompass the following subjects:

1. What the knowledge program is designed to do and why
2. What the major business entities are and how they relate
3. How to describe the daily operational work rules
4. How current business processes and information will be documented by the business operatives themselves
5. Examples of how business processes, rules, and information can be improved

The key to the success of this training activity is a *buy in* from business managers, project by project, throughout the company to affirm their responsibility for the knowledge transition.

Each business process must have a steward who will present to management and peers the results of an architected analysis. When managers are given this attention and allowed participation in structured analysis, there is evidence that the entire company takes on a new enthusiasm and that productivity increases. The benefits of *attention psychology* are as effective today as in the Western Electric Hawthorne Works' management study.

During the training process, the knowledge board formulates the information architecture to describe business processes, standards, and related functions of the company. The current company information reports, business functions, and rules are documented. The entire series of steps could take a company one to two years to complete. Modular system training releases the creative force of managers and operatives. It clarifies how each part of the work force interacts with the whole. The project-by-project training produces a productivity far more effective than a top-down planning or financial budget process.

The project-by-project architecture training may also be less costly and more productive than mass training because what is learned can be immediately practiced by improving existing systems.

SUMMARY

The key knowledge implementation steps are as follows:

1. Establish the knowledge board organization.
2. Select and assign key management responsibility to support the information program.

3. Create the knowledge planning library facility.
4. Establish the information architecture standards.
5. Select the technique for describing the business model.
6. Train selected staff in the business model and rule construction techniques.
7. Select the automated information encyclopedia and dictionary software.
8. Commence work on the business enterprise prototype.
9. Define the current business in terms of the current system.
10. Define existing automated support for business work that exists and any potential improvements.
11. Select and design an information architecture platform.
12. Compare business process needs with the total business rules and measurements.
13. Create modular building blocks using standards.
14. Use logical information modules to describe relational data base tables.
15. Select programming languages/standards.
16. Create modular computer functions to edit, update, process, and display knowledge.

There are, of course, many other decisions required for a knowledge project implementation. Each company will have its unique decisions to make. However, only after the knowledge architecture is in place should management entertain proposals for hardware, programming languages, networks, and other software changes.

The knowledge architecture is the master index and the overall platform for planning automation so that operatives can maintain control and understand what the global system is about. A framework is created as a separate entity so that any system change can be evaluated relative to its impact prior to any implementation. The physical system construction is a mirror image of its architecture.

Business enterprises are rapidly shifting from heavily tiered line and staff structures to more flat, distributed organizations. As more functions become automated, knowledge workers will increasingly automate their (mental) activities. Managers must spend more time to coordinate, plan, and mediate problems, rather than to disseminate data. Finding and relating information quickly will be a high priority. Management jobs will have to be redefined, and compensation has to be redistributed based on the contribution to knowledge.

Automated control must be inserted where humans can fail. The complexity of subject relationships is too much for humans to comprehend or remember without automated knowledge tools to prompt existing relationships.

Chapter 9

Business Knowledge ROI

INTRODUCTION

This chapter assumes that a business has created a knowledge asset. The knowledge board is in place. The knowledge architecture is in use. The knowledge migration is under way. The resource is in place.

Management will ask, "How does the company use this highly organized resource and keep it organized and up-to-date?"

Clearly, general business objectives will continue to exist and include some of the following changes of state:

Increase sales
Create new products
Improve product quality
Improve services
Find new markets
Improve profits
Increase productivity
Increase performance
Increase asset utilization
Lower functional costs
Improve vendor alliances

Whether the business is measured as a return on investment, assets, or equity, the knowledge base must be pursued to various levels of detail to determine and establish courses of strategic action.

Managers must insist that the knowledge base be updated in a systematic and consistent way. A proactive system for the examination of information must replace the reactive ad hoc approach. Major strategic pursuits can affect the ROI on information and the performance of individuals:

1. Business profit measurement
2. Business function costs
3. Product features, quality, and services
4. Business resource coupling (alliances)
5. Human resource recognition

Each of the preceding areas requires a presentation of information detail that focuses on

1. Responsibility for the knowledge collection
2. Distribution of the knowledge
3. Relationships between subjects
4. Business rules applied to subjects

This chapter describes a systematic knowledge review system that is necessary if an ROI on the knowledge base is to be realized.

An overriding idea is to generate an alliance between the internal business units and the external business resources with which the company transacts business. Cooperative efforts are the essence of profitability. The more of these ventures and relationships that can be maintained for the mutual interest of all members, the more profits can be generated. The realization of business members' profit contribution is dependent on their shared intelligence and their interactive relationships.

Note: The business that gathers intelligence and shares it as a service to its clients can achieve a leading strategic advantage to lock out competitors and lock in markets.

BUSINESS MEASUREMENTS

Figure 9.1 relates the major subjects and entities that interact in a typical business cycle.

Both information and product transfers are necessary between the various resources in the business cycle. One of the objectives of the business network is to maximize the physical volume and to accelerate the velocity of

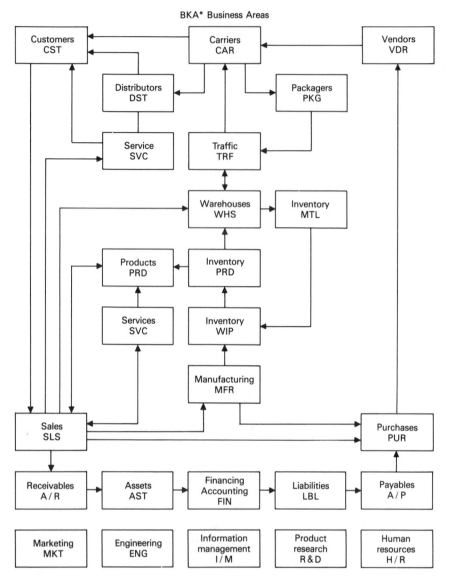

FIGURE 9.1   BKA business areas.

products. To the extent that the overall business cycle velocity can be increased, more profits can accrue to all parties provided those parties have status information pertaining to the transactions involved.

A large part of business information is produced for and about the flow in Figure 9.1. The business cycle pipeline must have the ability to expand and contract with volume. High-velocity information transfer facilitates human control. The measurements related to the physical process are major segments of the business knowledge base.

The measurement of the productivity of information is one of the most complex of business activities. Clearly, there are some companies that produce a volume of information at various data levels but do not use it effectively. One of the major reasons information is not used constructively is that it is not related, organized, controlled, or accessible. Those receiving it are not required to explain its meaning or to indicate what action to maximize profits should be invoked. Some operatives are not even aware of what the measurements mean or how they interact.

When measurement criteria are not established to show acceptable deviations from plans, standards, or expectations, information is just too much data. Business operatives viewing displays/reports are expected to use and act upon them. They must be trained in what exceptions can exist, how to detect them, and what action rules to invoke when they occur.

Typically, management mistakenly assumes that "experienced" egos know exactly what to do. More frequently, independent knee-jerk actions take place because things are too complex to remember or figure out.

Business measurements are directly related to the business measurement units (BMUs). Some examples of these measurements are as follows:

(BMU)	RESOURCES	MEASUREMENTS
Sales	Product	Rate of sale
Sales	Customer	Sales plan deviation
Purchasing	Vendor	Receipt days deviation
Purchasing	Product	Quote/invoice variance
Inventory	Product	Turnover
Inventory	Product	Cost to inventory
Transport	Carrier	Service days deviation
Transport	Product	Cost per distance
Manufacturing	Product	Unit cost variance
Manufacturing	Labor	Labor cost variance
Payroll	Employee class	Department budget variance
Payroll	Benefit class	Department budget variance
Supplies	Supply type	Supply type use variance
Supplies	Supply type	Department $ variance

In each of the preceding examples, management is expected to have established operating norms. When variances occur, they must be explained, and corrective action rules must be communicated.

The critical measurements for the total business cycle (Figure 9.1) must be continually reappraised to ensure that they represent the most critical success factors (CSFs) of the business. Measurements are frequently discovered to be inappropriate in light of changes in business relationships.

It is clear that hundreds of measurements for every aspect of a business can be invoked; however, most businesses can operate successfully using only a few key figures and only periodic snapshots of many others.

Yet, many businesses continue to produce volumes of measurements that cannot be explained. There will probably always be some margin of disagreement as to what is critical and what is not a critical measurement.

There are, however, some general considerations when evaluating measurements:

- If the measurements are single level (relating to only one subject), few insights will occur.
- If the quality of information is not adequate, then operatives will fail to maximize their profit-making potential.
- If the volume of information is too large, then operatives will be too overloaded to perform.
- If the time period that the information encompasses is too short, then overreaction can occur.
- If the time period that the information encompasses is too long, then no reaction may occur.
- If information reporting is too frequent, then business operatives' timing can be flawed.
- If information reporting is too infrequent, then business operatives may not be able to act quickly.

For the preceding reasons, the measurements of the business cycle (volume and velocity) must be chosen carefully. These measurements do not stand alone for their own sake. Their purpose is to expose adjustments for regulating the overall flow, thereby maximizing profits.

The mere exposure of measurements does not guarantee their recipients will react, or more importantly, *act together*, to regulate the transaction velocity. Businesses often allow department managers to request volumes of uncoordinated data reports and to create adjustments that do not maximize the flow of the business control cycle.

Therefore, managers must ensure the following:

1. All measurements relate to a complete *command and control* system for the total business. No gaps in the business cycle (Figure 9.1) can be allowed.
2. All measurements must have supporting response rules and operating policies to define what the operative is expected to do when each variance and deviation is encountered.

Typically, business reports are produced without displaying the expected actions or the options on the reports. Somehow the recipient is assumed to know precisely how to respond under any/all circumstances that can arise. Most report recipients are not even required to record (or review) their actions that are triggered by the reports. Few actions are documented. Compartmentalization continues.

An example of the need for supplemental reporting is appropriate. Consider a sales rate report *without* supplemental data:

THIS WEEK	LAST WEEK	RATE OF CHANGE
Sales $110,000	$100,000	10%
Location A		
Product class XCL		
Product X		
Quantity 110	100	10%
Sales $90,000	$100,000	−10%
Location B		
Product class XCL		
Product X		
Quantity 100	100	0%

This reporting of the rate of sale means little to the business operative. The obvious question is, why did the resulting sales deviate between the two locations?

The question can be supported if the deviation is put on the report itself. For example, consider the following:

- Advertising in location A was increased by 10 percent.
- Sales bonuses were increased by 5 percent at location A.
- A competitive store opened near location B.
- Prices were reduced by 10 percent at location B.

What rules should be applied under the preceding circumstances? Without displayed rules, management cannot be expected to know what works under these conditions. Traditionally, management would search out multiple reports to review the facts and inventory at location B. The combinations of data reporting are too large to allow ad hoc reporting or ad hoc reactions to take place.

Information value is measured by how quickly each profit variance can be related to its cause or rule. Unless managers are to structure and track information reporting and related action rules, the productivity of information cannot be evaluated.

Compound measurements further complicate the search for the key determinants of the optimum information mix. For example, because all of the business subjects and entities are connected to the flow of events in the business cycle,

- Sales relate to purchases/receivables.
- Sales relate to inventory/payables.
- Purchases relate to inventory.
- Inventory relates to cash/payables.
- Payroll relates to sales.

The measurement of relationships between BMU subjects—cause and effect—may be too complex for any company to control totally.

As each of the BMU relationships is established, corresponding business rules can be created. These interactive BMUs belong on business reports to trigger management analysis. The actions to be taken, based on the movement of BMU value relations, must always be displayed.

Traditionally, companies do not display alternate action rules.

The results of the action also must be recorded so that experience is not lost. *No learning can be reinforced if conditions, rules, and actions and responses are not exposed.*

Clearly, the entire business performance hinges on the critical profit measurements and rule structures that are in place. All business information detail must drive upward to BMU profit subjects.

The alternative to a profit-oriented architecture is a hodgepodge of uncoordinated actions.

BUSINESS FUNCTION UNIT COSTS

One of the current myths of automation is that computerization always means lower unit costs or provides better accuracy. In many cases, data input automation only results in saving a few clericals, which are rehired at higher job levels to keep extraneous data flowing for marginally effective functions.

Federal government reporting demands are an example of an overloading effect on many businesses. Reports can be required in six different sequences to produce employee information that is seldom used. What was once thought to be of prime importance has long since been abandoned, but the reporting continues.

For the enterprise to further benefit from the knowledge asset, it is necessary to undertake a meticulous cost examination of every business function, activity, and rule described in the migration (Chapter 8).

The first and foremost question is whether the function is needed at all. Then the question is, How can its cost be reduced or absorbed? This examination is a continuous activity because new, unneeded, or duplicate functions can slip unnoticed into the total operation.

The review of business functions also involves the examination of improved technology, methods, and standards. The methods can address both company internal functions and their interaction with external resource functions.

Electronic Data Interchange (EDI)

One of the more significant business investments in functional cost reduction is called *electronic data interchange* (EDI). EDI is the use of computers and data transmission facilities to deliver order and related information between buyers and sellers of products and services.

EDI relies on highly standardized and formatted messages that are switched from a sender to a receiver at computer speeds to reduce the costs of cumbersome manual handling of nonstandard paper documents. EDI systems have been in operation since the late 1960s but have gone virtually unnoticed by many managers. They were usually operated by single companies for specific business applications. Intercompany communications did not develop rapidly in part because every company had its own information architecture and formats. The business transaction translation problem was a major barrier without standards.

EDI standards were intially developed in 1975 by the Transport Data Coordinating Committee (TDCC), a nonprofit association of transport companies. EDI eliminated many costs involved in transportation tariff and rate filing information. In the late 1970s, EDI standards were extended to the airline, railroad, shipping, and trucking industries. Standards were then developed for the grocery industry and labeled EDI_UCS. Various standard subsets were extended to the warehousing industry and labeled WINS.

In association with the TDCC, the American National Standards Institute (ANSI) developed the X12 standard for business data interchange; it is a basic purchase order and invoice system.

Since these initially slow developments, the pace has quickened. Many major associations have joined the rush to standards. The Automotive Industry Action Group (AIAG) is moving the automobile industry quickly toward a single standard so that over 30,000 suppliers can communicate electronically with their customers using a single format.

Other industry associations have joined in the exercise to adopt at least a part of the ANSI X12 standards:

- EDX   Electrical industry
- NACHA   Banking industry
- ACCS   Metals industry
- NIDA   National Industrial Distributors Association
- ASMMA   American Supply & Machinery Association
- CIDX   Chemical industry
- NRMA   National Retail Merchants Association

The expectations are high that the following benefits can be achieved:

- Lower operating costs
- Reduced data entry errors and reentry costs
- Faster cash flows and floats
- Higher accuracy
- Lower warehouse costs (just-in-time)

- Lower inventory levels and lead times
- Minimized clerical staff
- Increased market competition and customer services
- Reduced system development time
- Paper cost savings

The movement to EDI is facilitated by many third-party computer service vendors, who anticipate a billion-dollar industry by the 1990s. Among these vendors are

- McDonnell Douglas (EDI Net)
- GE Information Services (Transnet)
- Informatic General Corporation (Ordernet)
- Control Data Corporation (Redinet)
- Transettlements, Inc.
- Railinc. Corporation (Train II)
- IBM (IN)

Some of these third parties may prefer to stay within an industry-oriented market, while others may prefer to cross industries in order to connect industries such as government agencies, banks, carriers, vendors, customers, dealers, and many ancillary industry services.

For the enthusiasm to come to fruition, managers will have to recognize the need for describing their business functions in an architected and standard format, both within their own business and in conformity with evolving industry standards. An ad hoc approach to business functions and their rules and information is rapidly becoming obsolete in profitable firms.

PRODUCT QUALITY AND SERVICE

The business cycle measurements and business unit costs are critical to keeping management aware of the status of the enterprise. However, knowledge and information about the business products are key to what must be done to improve profits.

Whether the business product is a tangible item, a service, or a combination of both, product knowledge is the key to profits. The product is referenced by every aspect of the business. While various departmental managements may be transfixed (or obsessed) by technology and automation, the product itself must be the key focus of the company.

The successful enterprise is faced with continual challenges

1. To continue to improve current products
2. To continue to introduce new products

Recently, the product lifetime has shortened while preproduct development time has lengthened. Product uniqueness frequently adds to the development time/cost that must be recovered by a high price before clone-makers copy and compete.

Meanwhile, makers of standard, non-unique products chisel away at reducing the costs of

- Manufacturing
- Marketing
- Distribution

until the weakest fail.

In all cases, the product information base is a predominant key to profits. Almost every arm of the business depends on having immediate and up-to-date access to every aspect of the business products.

No sales representative can be knowledgeable in more than a small fraction of the company products. Yet, a knowledge tool to access any phase or detail about any product gives the sales representative a competitive advantage in technical accuracy that is bound to impress the client.

No purchasing agent can remember all of the product properties that are required in a purchase. A knowledge tool, which provides accessible and correct product information, can help to ensure product quality across all purchased lines.

Product knowledge also applies to competitors' products and their point-for-point comparisons to the internal business products. This type of information gives sales, purchasing, and engineering staffs a distinct advantage.

Product knowledge and information extend far beyond the standard examples in most texts. Some product attributes are as follows:

Product identification
Product description
Product quantity/pricing
Product quantity/costing
Product vendors
Product competitors
Product standards
Product failures
Product quality/purity
Product quantities on hand
Product assemblies
Product drawings/specifications
Product parts
Product substitutions
Product interchangeability
Product laws/liability/warranty

Product safety
Product requests/complaints

When knowledge and its information are carried to such depth and are readily accessible, the business credibility can be an asset that will automatically attract customers. Where this type of information is divulged with discretion, the business customer base is strengthened. A related facility is the ability to record complaints and requests that can assist in product upgrading or new product introductions.

Increasingly, product components are being standardized to allow new products to be constructed from previously developed parts. It is no secret that standard components made for one product can readily be used in/for another product, reducing both development and production costs. The substitutability factor is an important element in product information.

Product knowledge is increasingly being integrated with the use of artificial intelligence (AI). More and more expert rule alternatives are being captured to work human knowledge against product relationships and rules to produce specific results.

There is little question that business product knowledge is a major subject to be architected and shared. Duplicate islands of compartmentalized product information cannot be allowed to impede company and group productivity. Individualized ownership of information can no longer be permitted. When Joe left, it all went with him!

EXTERNAL INFORMATION COUPLING

Group productivity must be extended beyond the internal departments of a business. The win-win strategy is supported when multiple businesses are able to share common objectives and utilize common information to meet those objectives.

What previously was considered proprietary or competitive information can be considered mutually shareable. Knowledge shared between the company and its vendors, competitors, customers, contractors, lawyers, accountants, carriers, insurers, etc., makes a major difference in profits.

For example, business product sales forecasts of one company can be vital to the lead time required for their prime vendors or manufacturers. A future forecast of a metal shortage by a manufacturer can be critical for a business that buys for inventory. Various arrangements by a customer to finance inventory for the manufacturer are not a new concept.

An objective is to establish and hold future costs. The chain extends from raw material sources through manufacturing and labor availability to carriers, the distributor, and the end-point consumer. Without integrated knowledge chains and connections about these stages in the business cycle, economies would widely fluctuate, and chaos would prevail.

The natural laws of resource availability, national policy, foreign laws, and business rules (laws) all are related to the integration of worldwide knowledge. The business enterprise must consider how tightly it needs to couple certain external knowledge and its internal knowledge bases. Each business needs to plan what intelligence information it must track and the cost of that tracking. Whether a business requires market, product commodities, news, legal, medical, or other types of information, it is critical to couple it to the business measurement units.

Competitive airlines (foreign and domestic) sharing massive flight, maintenance, and reservation information systems is an example of synergistic cost reduction and competitive advantage.

Similar cooperative opportunities between companies are limited only by the ingenuity of their managements. New technology has provided the real opportunity for *affiliate thinking*. The key to this affiliation is external information coupling, which in turn requires standardized

1. Accounting architecture
2. Information architecture
3. Work (rule) architecture
4. Logistics architecture

prior to implementing new technology. Only then is it time to consider

1. Hardware architecture
2. Operations software
3. Networks/hardware/software techniques

SUMMARY

The cost of planning, standardizing, and documenting the business knowledge architecture is miniscule compared to the implementation cost of installing the physical technology. If a technology base is laid before the architecture is synchronized, the first change can be like breaking up concrete foundations.

If a business cannot get its own in-house knowledge and information organized, modularized, and architected along the BKA lines previously described, it may be only a matter of time before it is unable to interact strategically with external corporate resources. The day of the information planner, architect, and engineer has arrived, and that person is the *business manager* equipped with knowledge architecture and its supporting computerized tools.

Epilogue

American industry is confronted with the choice of automating knowledge or facing dwindling profits. If industry does not perfect its knowledge, information, activities, functions, and rules, there won't be any jobs in certain industries.

Foreign competition has demonstrated its capability to steal, clone, and manufacture as effectively as domestic U.S. businesses. The quality, work ethic, and lower wages of foreign competition have enabled it to penetrate the worldwide market share.

The portability and standardization of technology have enabled more and more human functions to be replaced by robotics, machines, and computing devices. Every part of the production process has been placed under intense scrutiny. Computer-assisted design and manufacturing has even been responsible for increasing the productivity of knowledge workers. The targets have obviously been the blue-collar functions that previously guided the sequential steps of the manufacturing process. Those sequential tasks have been converted into simultaneous computer-driven commands that the average human worker can hardly understand, let alone compete with.

Consequently, fewer and fewer people are assuming responsibility for more and more of those who cannot keep up with the thrust of technological change.

The next target is clearly (white-collar) middle-management knowledge translators. Just as the functions of manufacturing were decomposed in order to standardize robotic architecture, information, functions, and rules must be decomposed and standardized. The coupling of robotics, laser sensing, and information has already begun.

As the automation of white-collar jobs continues, it is not unusual to project a future of fewer jobs composed mainly of pushing a start button at 8 A.M. and a stop button at 5 P.M. The purpose of this book is not to evaluate whether the high-tech automation of business knowledge is a blessing or a curse. Information technology may well erode the American white-collar middle-class society while producing very competitive products. The automated result may be only a few good jobs that belong to genetically selected knowledge workers and a semiwelfare existence for the less educated masses.

A few companies are actively underway creating computerized tools to facilitate our next higher level of social progress based on business knowledge, information architecture and graphic integration. These new knowledge products are already creating software obsolescence.

The cost of knowledge tools will increase, but they will not automatically replace the creative mental work (activity) that a company must pursue to ensure that its software contributes to profitability.

Without an organized and automated business model, business knowledge, and rule architecture tools, the most elaborate new software will yield only a marginal return.

Without high caliber management understanding and involvement, a knowledge program will fail to return its investment. Without the right people and the correct techniques, little results can be expected.

Hopefully, this book has described enough about the need to invest in employees, training, and knowledge tools. Every company that undertakes a knowledge program may eventually apply its own unique methods. Immediate results cannot be expected, but the plans, responsibilities, and funding schedules must be created to ensure that the foundation is in place. Major outlays for computer hardware and software should be deferred until the knowledge architecture has been put in place to architect the existing system and identify existing gaps in work, rules, and information.

Just as the auto industry predicts that all of its plants must be rebuilt, reequipped, and retooled, business knowledge perception must also be restructured. The shell must be constructed.

There is simply no more room for the historical knowledge shantytowns, quick fix packages and throw-away software. Changes in company uniforms are no longer enough. The manipulation of financial assets, leveraged low-margin buy-outs, short-term investment speculation, and making money on paper assets do *not* facilitate productivity or performance.

In some companies, the movement has clearly been away from investing in productive assets. Historically, productivity has *not* been a major interest of American management. Institutional investor mentality prevails, demands immediate results, and inhibits long-term ventures in knowledge from taking hold. Some managers seek only to convert assets into short-term profits and immediate earnings.

Financial mentality typically defines people and information as overhead rather than as a value-added resource. Accounting overhead is consequently reduced as more people are replaced by machines. At some point, the few remaining low-cost temporary clericals will no longer compensate for the loss in strategic thinking. The *will to manage* the product is lost in the cost accounting paradigm. The knowledge asset, while intangible, is absolutely the most productive and important investment.

The focus of a knowledge architecture program is on profits, product quality, and customer service. Technology does not automatically produce profits. Technology only permits problems to be solved where the method of solution can be very accurately described:

What markets?	How to reward?
What products?	How to inspire?
What research?	How to train?
How to fund?	How to dismantle?
How to organize?	

The challenge of American middle management is analogous to the insect world. Fewer and fewer knowledge queens will forge heavily architected colonies in order to preserve and stimulate the productive instincts of future generations.

Many workers contribute to the preservation of the colony (enterprise) and are totally dependent on it for survival against external threats. Without selective (genetic) upgrading and adaptation to new technology, all species will give way to extinction.

> The business knowledge investment clearly must be the strategy.

Appendix 1

Definitions

BKA subject   A major business entity. A single object, idea, representation, person, place, or thing having a unique identity or name.

BKA subject relationship types   The joining of two or more *key* business subjects forms a concatenated string, new subject, or unique idea. A relationship type exists when strings have the same major subjects. In the search for information relationships, types help to focus the search for specific subjects and objects having the same subject-to-subject combination.

BKA subject types   Six classes/groups of key business subjects. Used to establish the scope of, structure of, and priority for information integration. Used to construct business information views, tables, and standard unit patterns.

1. BMT: business (profit) measurement type
2. BOT: business organization type
3. BLT: business location type
4. BRT: business resource type
5. BTT: business transaction type
6. BPT: business product type

BKA terminology types   Seven classes/groups of like *nonkey* business terms. Terms are used to modify and extend key business subjects. The types are used to establish and standardize the sequence and use of attributive terms.

1. EXT: extension control type
2. SCT: status control type
3. TPT: time period type
4. TFT: time frequency type
5. CVT: control verb type
6. UMT: unit of measurement type
7. VLT: value type

BLT, business location type   Business subject priority type 3. The physical location types of a business. Encapsulated physical business location relationships.

BMT, business measurement type   Business subject priority type 1. The major measurements of a business. The critical success (profit) factors of a business. The major assets or liabilities of a business. The highest level search keys of BKA information.

BOT, business organization type   Business subject priority type 2. The business organization entity types. Key responsibility areas of a business. Encapsulated organization of work relationships.

BPT, business product type   Business subject type 6. The products of the business. The services of the business. The product service relationships.

BRT, business resource type   Business subject priority type 4. External resources used by a business. Service channels engaged by a business. Assets utilized by a business.

BTT, business transaction type   Business subject priority type 5. Legal agreements, events and activities of the business. Communications between internal business units and/or external resources. Contracts and binders.

Business knowledge domains   The highest level of categorization for business knowledge. Consist of
  1. Subject domain
  2. Terminology domain
  3. Work domain
  4. Rule domain
  5. Information domain

Business subject attribute   A business subject has unique attributive terms, descriptors, or properties. A column member of a business subject table inherits the properties of its table's subject.

Business subject attribute value   A value of a business subject is the contents of a table's row-column intersection (cell value).

Business subject's domain   Consists of all of all the values of a business subject-extension (i.e., all of the cells in a column of a table).

CVT, control verb type   Terminology priority type 5. Consists of command operators that initiate and prescribe action in process. Consists of key verbs for defining and naming business work types and rule types.

EXT, extension control type   Terminology priority type 1. Object nouns that amplify/ extend business subject meanings. Attributive words that modify subject types 1–6.

Information types   Classifications/groups of meaningful collections of data:
  1. Tables/files/records
  2. Reports/displays
  3. Transactions
  4. Elements (data)

Knowledge levels   Corresponding levels of business knowledge specificity within each domain (global context to absolute detail):
  1. Types (categories/classifications)
  2. Lists (a list of unit/instances of type)
  3. Attributes (extension properties of a subject)
  4. Relationships (subject-to-subject associations)
  5. Statements (descriptive icons, phrases, formulas)

Rule types   Classifications for controlling like business rules:
  1. MRT: measurement rule type
  2. ORT: organization rule type
  3. LRT: location rule type
  4. RRT: resource rule type
  5. TRT: transaction rule type
  6. PRT: product rule type

SCT, status control type   Terminology priority type 2. Descriptors that stipulate/describe a condition of a subject. Attributive words to establish a subject status. The antithesis of a control type verb (CVT).

Subject table   An array of subject-extensions (columns) with rows of records having corresponding values at their intersections called *cells*.

TFT, time-frequency type   Terminology priority type 4. Descriptors that describe occurrences of a business subject *within* a time period. An attribute used to extend terminology type 3.

TPT, time period type   Terminology priority type 3. Descriptors that establish a time period in which a business event or subject occurs or exists. An attribute used to modify subject types 1–6.

UMT, unit of measurement type   Terminology priority type 6. Units by which a subject's value is measured. Attributes that quantify the value of an expression.

VLT, value type   Terminology priority type 7. The format by which the value is expressed. Integer, decimal, character, and number are value types.

Work types   Encapsulated clusters of like kinds of work to control (hierarchical) superior/subordinate relationship concepts:

1. MIS.missions
2. OBJ.objectives
3. GOL.goals
4. PLN.plans
5. PRJ.projects
6. PRC.processes
7. FNC. functions
8. ACT.activities
9. TSK.Tasks
10. CPU_JOBS
11. PRG_PROGRAMS
12. CPF_COMPUTER PROGRAM FUNCTIONS
13. CFM_COMPUTER PROGRAM MODULES

Appendix 2

Major Business Subjects by Type

BUSINESS SUBJECT MEASUREMENT TYPES

ACRONYM	MEASUREMENT_NAMES
SLS	Sales
PUR	Purchases
INV	Inventory
TRN	Transportation
ADV	Advertising
MKT	Marketing
PAY	Payroll
BFT	Benefits
EXP	Expenses
SPL	Supplies
INC	Income
PBT	Profit before taxes
TAX	Tax payable
PAT	Profit after taxes
CSH	Cash
A/R	Accounts receivable
EQP	Equipment
PLT	Plant
LND	Land
A/P	Accounts payable
STK	Stock
CAP	Capital

BUSINESS SUBJECT ORGANIZATION TYPES

ACRONYM	ORGANIZATION_NAMES
INC	Company
DIV	Division
PDL	Product line
MKT	Market
REG	Region
DST	District
DEP	Department
JCL	Job class
JOB	Job
PRC	Process
ACT	Activity
FNC	Function
CPJ	Computer job
PRG	Computer program
CPF	Computer program function

BUSINESS SUBJECT LOCATION TYPES

ACRONYM	LOCATION_NAMES
CTN_	COUNTRY_NAME
ST:_	STATE_NAME
PRV_	PROVINCE_NAME
CTY_	COUNTY_NAME
ZIP_	POSTAL_ZONE
CIT_	CITY_NAME
STR_	STREET_NAME
ST#_	STREET_IDN
BLD_	BUILDING_IDN
FLR_	FLOOR_IDN
ARN_	AREA_NAME
SEC_	SECTION_IDN
RM#_	ROOM_IDN
LV#_	LEVEL_IDN
BIN_	BIN_IDN
FIL_	FILE_IDN

BUSINESS SUBJECT RESOURCE TYPES

ACRONYM	RESOURCE_NAMES
DSC	Distribution channel
CST	Customer
DLR	Dealer
LIC	Licensee
OEM	Other eqp mfr
GOV	Government
FLT	Fleet

ACRONYM	RESOURCE_NAMES
ITC	Intracompany
AGT	Agent
PRC	Procurement channel
MFR	Manufacturer
VDR	Vendor (noncompany)
CTR	Contractor
SPL	Supplier (supplies)
PKG	Packager
CAR	Carrier
ISR	Insurer
BNK	Bank
STH	Stakeholder class
CPT	Competitor
STK	Stockholder
IVS	Investor
OWN	Owner
AFL	Affiliate
EMP	Employee
RGL	Regulator
CMU	Community
FAC	Facilities class
BLD	Building
DPT	Depot
F/F	Furniture/fixtures
VEH	Vehicles
CPU	Computers
TER	Terminals (display units)
CPY	Copiers
LND	Land
KNW	Knowledge class
PAT	Patents
DWG	Drawings
SFW	Software
STD	Standards
PCD	Procedures
PRG	Programs (computer)
FIL	Files
REC	Records
TBL	Tables (data)
SVC	Services
ITM	Items

BUSINESS SUBJECT TRANSACTION TYPES

ACRONYM	TRANSACTION_NAMES
INC_PRD_DTO	Product depot transfer order
INC_MTO	Material transfer order

ACRONYM	TRANSACTION_NAMES
INC_DLR_$DB	Company dealer debit
INC_CAP_APR	Company capital appropriation
INC_VDR_MTO	Company vendor material transfer order
INC_MFR_PDD	Company manufacturer purchase debit
INC_W/O	Company work order
INC_PRD_R/O	Company product repair order
INC_PRD_F/M	Company product file updates
INC_J/V	Company journal vouchers
DLR_S/O	Dealer sales order
DLR_F/M	Dealer file management
DLR_RTN	Dealer return
DLR_PMT	Dealer payment
DLR_B/O	Dealer back order
DLR_RFQ	Dealer request for quote
DLR_RMT	Dealer remittance
DLR_CTR	Dealer contract
DLR_SHP	Dealer shipment
DLR_QTE	Dealer quote
DLR_IVC	Dealer invoice
VDR_F/M	Vendor file management
VDR_PMT	Vendor payment
VDR_RTN	Vendor return
VDR_SHP	Vendor shipment
VDR_CTR	Vendor contract
VDR_QTE	Vendor quote
VDR_RMT	Vendor remittance
VDR_RFQ	Vendor request for quote
VDR_IVC	Vendor invoice
VDR_B/O	Vendor backorder
VDR_P/O	Vendor purchase order
CAR_B/L	Carrier bill of lading
CAR_T/O	Carrier transport order
CAR_QTE	Carrier quote
CAR_F/M	Carrier file updates
CAR_RMT	Carrier remittance
CAR_PMT	Carrier payment
CAR_IVC	Carrier invoice
PKG_F/M	Packager file update
PKG_SHP	Packager shipment
PKG_PMT	Packager payment
PKG_P/O_REC	Packager P/O receipt
PKG_IVC	Packager invoice
PKG_CTR	Packager contract
EMP_F/M	Employee file update
EMP_PAY_RTE	Employee pay rate
EMP_RET	Employee retirement
EMP_SAV	Employee savings

ACRONYM	TRANSACTION_NAMES
EMP_HRS	Employee hours
EMP_BFT	Employee benefits

BUSINESS SUBJECT PRODUCT TYPES

ACRONYM	PRODUCT_NAMES
PCL	Product class (strata)
PRD	Products
MOD	Models
ASM	Assemblies
KIT	Kits
PTS	Parts

Appendix 3

Business Terminology by Type

BUSINESS EXTENSION TYPES

ACRONYM	EXTENSION_NAME
A/C	Account
ACR	Acronym
ACT	Activity
ADJ	Adjustment
ADR	Address
AIR	Air
AMH	Auto materials handling
ANV	Anniversary
APT	Apartment
ARA	Area
ATH	Author
ATR	Attribute
AUT	Austria
B/I	Batch interface
B/M	Bill of material
BAS	Base
BAT	Batch
BDG	Badge
BET	Business extension type
BFR	Beneficiary
BIL	Billing

ACRONYM	EXTENSION_NAME
BKN	Breakdown
BLC	Block
BLK	Blanket (order)
BLT	Business location type
BMT	Business measurement type
BOT	Business organization type
BOX	Box
BPT	Business product type
BSN	Business
BTH	Birth
BTT	Business transaction type
BU/	Buyer
CAD	Computer-assisted design
CAE	Computer-aided engineering
CAL	Calendar
CAM	Computer-aided manufacturing
CAN	Canada
CCN	Cost change notice
CHK	Check
CHN	China
CIC	Communication control system
CIM	Computer-integrated manufacturing
CIT	City
CJB	Computer job
CL1	Class 1 order
CL2	Class 2 order
CL3	Class 3 order
CL4	Class 4 order
CLR	Clerical
CLS	Class
CMD	Commodity
CMF	Computer master functions
COG	Cost of goods
COL	Column
COM	Commission
CPT	Competitor
CPU	Computer processing unit
CPY	Copy
CTG	Casting
CTL	Control device
CTZ	Citizen
CTX	Context
CVG	Coverage
CYC	Cycle
D&B	Dun & Bradstreet
D/B	Data base
DCL	Demand class

ACRONYM	EXTENSION_NAME
DGR	Degree
DIM	Dimensions
DN/	Down
DOM	Domestic
DPT	Depot
DRP	Distribution requirements plan
DSC	Description
DWG	Drawing
EDI	Electronic data interchange
EDU	Education
EEO	Equal employment opportunity
ELE	Data element
EMA	Enterprise MGT architecture
EMR	Emergency
EOQ	Economic order quantity
ERR	Error
EXE	Executive
EXM	Exempt
EXT	Extension term name
ECT	Extension control type
FAC	Facility
FCH	Fiche
FCT	Forecast
FET	Federal excise tax
FGN	Foreign
FIL	File
FLD	Field
FLM	Film
FLT	Fleet
FMP	Fast-moving parts
FNC	Function
FNL	Final
FNM	First name
FRM	Form
FRN	France
FRT	Freight
G/L	General ledger
G/M	Gross margin
GOL	Goals
GOV	Government
GPH	Graph
GRD	Grade
GRP	Group
GRS	Gross
GT>	Greater than
HCP	Handicapped
HDL	Handling

ACRONYM	EXTENSION_NAME
HIR	Hire
HOM	Home
IDN	Identification number
IFR	Information references
IFT	Information type
INC	Incorporation
INF	Information
INS	Insurance
IRC	Interregion communication
ISA	Info systems architecture
ISO	International Org for Standards
ITA	Italy
ITR	Interest
IVT	Investments
JFX	Jigfix
JIT	Just in time
JNL	Journal
JOB	Job
JPN	Japan
KEY	Key
L/S	Linkage section
LAN	Local area network
LBR	Labor
LDR	Leader
LF<	Left
LGC	Logic
LIA	Liability
LIN	Line
LIS	List
LNE	Lane
LNM	Last name
LT<	Less than
LTR	Letter
LTT	Letter text
LVL	Level
LYF	Layoff
M/L	Medical leave
M/S	Marital status
MAD	Mean average deviation
MAN	Manual
MAP	MFR automation protocol
MDL	Model
MDM	Modem
MEM	Memorandum
MFG	Manufacturing
MGR	Manager
MGT	Management

ACRONYM	EXTENSION_NAME
MHD	Method
MIL	Military
MIS	Management info systems
MJR	Major
MLT	Multiple
MNM	Middle name
MNR	Minor
MNU	Menu
MOD	Module
M&C	Manufacturing and control
MSC	Miscellaneous
MSG	Message
MTL	Material
MUX	Multiplexer
NAM	Name
NET	Net
NNM	Nickname
NON	Not
NOR	Norway
NOS	Network operating system
OBJ	Object
OCN	Ocean
OPR	Operative
OPS	Operations
ORA	Oracle
ORI	Origin
OSI	Open systems interconnection
OSI_APL	OSI_APPLICATION #7LEVEL
OSI_LNK	OSI_DATALINK #2LEVEL
OSI_NET	OSI_NETWORK #3LEVEL
OSI_PHY	OSI_PHYSICAL #1LEVEL
OSI_PRS	OSI_PRESENTATION #6LEVEL
OSI_SES	OSI_SESSION #5LEVEL
OSI_TRN	OSI_TRANSPORTATION #4LEVEL
OTP	Output
OVH	Overhead
P&L	Profit and loss
P/L	Packing list
PAK	Package
PAL	Pallet
PAY	Pay
PCN	Price change notice
PCT	Percentage
PCY	Policy
PSN	Personal
PFR	Performance
PFX	Prefix

ACRONYM	EXTENSION_NAME
PLN	Plan
PMM	Premium
PMT	Payment
POI	Point of impact
POR	Point of receipt
POS	Point of sale
PRG	Program
PRJ	Project
PRO	Professional
PRP	Property
PRV	Previous
PST	Packing station
QRY	Query
RAC	Race
RAK	Rack
RAM	Random access memory
REA	Reason
REF	Reference
RFG	Report file generator
RFR	Referred
REL	Relationship
RHR	Rehire
RJE	Remote job entry
RLA	Rule attribute
RLR	Rule reference
RLS	Rule statement
RLT	Rule type
RMG	Remaining
RNG	Range
ROI	Return on investment
ROM	Read only memory
ROP	Reorder point
ROW	Row
RPT	Report
RT>	Right
RTE	Rate
RTM	Retirement
RUL	Rule
S/M	Sell multiple
S/R	Sales rate
S/S	Safety stock
SAA	Systems application architecture
SAL	Salary
SBJ	Subject
SEA	Seasonal
SEG	Segment
SEN	Seniority

ACRONYM	EXTENSION_NAME
SEX	Sex
SFX	Suffix
SGL	Single
SHM	Shipment
SHP	Shipper
SIZ	Size
SKU	Stockkeeping unit
SNA	System network architecture
SPL	Special
SPS	Spouse
SPV	Supervisor
SQC	SQL*CALC
SQF	SQL*FORMS
SQP	SQL*PLUS
SQR	SQL*REPORT
SRC	Source
SSN	Social security number
ST:	State
STA	Status
STD	Standard
STK	Stock
STM	Statement
STR	Street
SUB	Substitutes
SVC	Services
SWE	Sweden
T/D	Trade discount
TAR	Tariffs
TAX	Tax
TBL	Table
TCF	Transparent computing facility
TCP	Transmission control protocol
TCU	Time class unit
TEC	Technician
TEH	Czechoslovakia
TEL	Telephone
TFU	Time frequency units
TIC	Ticket
TLT	Title
TLG	Tooling
TMU	Time measurement unit
TOP	Technical and office protocol
TOP	Technical office products
TRK	Truck
TRM	Terms
TRS	Transaction
TSK	Task

ACRONYM	EXTENSION_NAME
TTL	Total
TWX	Transmission type
TXT	Text
TYP	Type
UOM	Units of measurement
UP/	Upward
UPS	United Parcel, Inc.
URS	Union of Soviet Socialist Rep
USA	United States of America
VAL	Value
VAR	Variance
VCH	Voucher
VDT	Video display terminal
VNM	Vietnam
VOC	Voice
W-4	W-4
WKA	Work attribute
WKR	Work reference
WKT	Work type
WRK	Work
ZIP	Zip code
ZON	Zone

BUSINESS STATUS TYPES

ACRONYM	STATUS_UNIT_NAME
$CR	Credited
$DB	Debited
ABE	Abnormal ended
ABV	Abbreviated
ACT	Active
ADJ	Adjusted
ADR	Addressed
ADV	Advertised
AFS	Available for sale
AGD	Aged
ALL	All inclusive
ALO	Allocated
ALT	Altered
ANR	Allocated not released
AOK	Satisfactory
APV	Approved
ASG	Assigned
ASM	Assembled
ATH	Authorized
ATV	Active

ACRONYM	STATUS_UNIT_NAME
AUD	Audited
AUT	Automated
AVG	Averaged
B/O	Back-ordered
BAT	Batched
BEG	Begun
BGT	Budgeted
BOK	Booked
BUF	Buffered
BUP	Backed up
BWD	Backward direction
CCL	Canceled
CFR	Confirmed
CHG	Changed
CLC	Calculated
CLM	Claimed
CLS	Classified
CMT	Committed
CNT	Counted
COR	Corrected
CPL	Completed
CMP	Complied
CPY	Copied
CRE	Created
CRG	Charged
CSD	Consolidated
CTL	Controlled
DMG	Damaged
DCD	Deceased
DCR	Decreased
DCT	Discounted
DEF	Defective
DEL	Deleted
DES	Described
DFC	Defective
DLV	Delivered
DSP	Displayed
DUE	Due
EDT	Edited
END	Ended
EQ=	Equals
EST	Estimated
EVL	Evaluated
EXE	Executed
FCT	Forecasted
FIL	Filed
FMR	Former

ACRONYM	STATUS_UNIT_NAME
FOB	Free on board
FRZ	Frozen
FUT	Future
FWD	Forward direction
HAZ	Hazardous
HCP	Handicapped
HLT	Halted
HST	History
IAC	Inactivated
ICL	Included
ICR	Increased
INB	Inbound
INO	Invoiced not ordered
INP	Invoiced not paid
INR	Invoiced not received
INT	Initiated
IPR	In process
ISP	Inspected
ITS	Intransit
IVC	Invoiced
KYD	Keyed
LBL	Labeled
LCH	Lunch
LDD	Loaded
LDT	Lead time
LKD	Linked
LLT	Less lead time
LST	Last
LTL	Less than truckload
MAX	Maximized
MDN	Marked down
MEC	Mechanized
MIN	Minimized
MTR	Monitored
MUP	Marked up
N/A	Not applicable
N/C	No charge
NAF	Not available for sale
NAK	Not acknowledged
NCH	No change
NCO	No cost
NDX	Indexed
NEW	Newly created
NGO	Negotiated
NID	Not identified
NLA	No longer available
NOH	Not on hand

ACRONYM	STATUS_UNIT_NAME
NOK	Not satisfactory
NOO	Not on order
NRL	Not released
NRT	Not returnable
NSK	Not stocked
NSP	Not shipped
O/H	On hand
O/L	On line
O/O	On order
O/S	Over or short
ONI	Ordered not invoiced
ONR	Ordered not received
OPR	Operational
OTB	Outbound
OVR	Overridden
P/D	Past due date
PD/	Paid
PKD	Packed
PLN	Planned
PML	Purchased multiple
PPD	Prepaid
PPK	Prepacked
PRC	Processed
PRI	Primary
PRM	Promised
PRX	Proximity
PTD	Printed
QRY	Queried
QTD	Quoted
REC	Received
REJ	Rejected
REL	Related
REQ	Requisitioned
REV	Reviewed
RFB	Refurbished
RFU	Ready for use
RLS	Released
RMT	Remitted
RNI	Received not invoiced
RNO	Received not ordered
RNS	Received not stored
RPR	Repaired
RSH	Rush
RST	Restricted
RSV	Reserved
RTD	Retired
RTI	Return to inventory

ACRONYM	STATUS_UNIT_NAME
RTV	Return to vendor
RVD	Revised
S/D	Ship direct to user
SCD	Scheduled
SCR	Scrapped
SCT	Status control type
SEL	Selected
SEP	Separated
SEQ	Sequenced
SHK	Shrunken
SHT	Short
SML	Sold multiple
SNS	Sold not shipped
SPD	Shipped
SRT	Sorted
STO	Stored
SUM	Summarized
SUS	Suspended
TER	Terminated
TTL	Totaled
UPD	Updated
VLD	Validated
W/O	Without
WKD	Worked
XCH	Exchanged
XCL	Excluded
XCO	Without a cost
XPR	Without a price

Appendix 4

Business Work, Rule, and Information Type Definitions

WORK TYPE DEFINITIONS

WKT   Work type name. Level of work: a hierarchy of encapsulation.

MIS   Missions. Category of work: enduring long-term statements of business intent.

OBJ   Objectives. Category of work: planned change in status of business subject to support missions.

GOL   Goals. Category of work: a specific target. Measurable as a value. Identified by a time period or date.

PRJ   Projects. Category of work: collection of one-time activities. Tasks to achieve a goal.

PRC   Processes. Category of work: clusters of like work activities and functions.

ACT   Activities. Category of work: consists of (mental) analysis using information.

FNC   Function. Category of work: ongoing (physical) human tasks. Repetitive using discrete rules.

TSK   Task. Category of work: discrete work units. Part of a job function.

JOB   Job. Category of work: combination of related human functions, activities, and tasks.

CJB   COMPUTER_JOB. Category of work: computer program/program string combination of execution of sequences.

PRG   Computer program. Category of work: a group of computer commands and functional instructions to accomplish a computer job.

CMF   Computer master function. Category of work: a cluster of computer commands. A subunit of computer program unit: edit, validate, file, update, execute, display, print, etc.

RULE TYPE DEFINITIONS

RLT   Rule type name. Levels of rules: a hierarchy of rule encapsulation.

MRT   Measurement rule type. Category of rules: describe how to measure business subjects.

RULE TYPE DEFINITIONS

ORT   Organization rule type. Category of rules: describe how business work is organized.

LRT   Location rule type. Category of rules: describe where organization and its facilities are located.

RRT   Resource rule type. Category of rules: describe regulation/relationships between company and its resource units.

TRT   Transaction rule type. Category of rules: describe the transactions between company and its resources.

PRT   Product rule type. Category of rules: describe the products of the business.

INFORMATION TYPE DEFINITIONS

IFT   Information types. Levels of information: a hierarchy of information encapsulation.

DBT   Data base type. A category for clustering data segments, records, or segments.

DBS   Data segment type. A category for grouping related data elements.

DST   Display screen type. A category for groups of data elements displayed together on video screens (VDT).

FIL   File type. A category for groups of related data records about a subject.

REC   Record type. A category for data elements that relate to a subject.

RPT   Report type. A category of collections of printed data elements.

TRS   Transaction type. A category of data elements needed for a contract and to record an event.

TBL   Table type. A category for data element collections that correlate subject pairs.

ELE   Data element type. A class of a subject (or string of related subject/term combinations). The lowest descriptive level for an information unit.

Appendix 5

References

APPLEGATE, L. M. "Information Technology and Tomorrow's Manager." *Harvard Business Rev.*, No. 6, Nov.-Dec. 1988.

DATE, C. J. *An Introduction to Data Base Systems.* Reading, Mass.: Addison-Wesley, 1975.

DAWKINS, R. *The Selfish Gene.* New York: Oxford University Press, 1976.

DAWKINS, R. *The Extended Phenotype.* New York: Oxford University Press, 1982.

DONOVAN, J. J. "Beyond Chief Information Officer to Network Manager." *Harvard Business Rev.*, No. 5, Sept.-Oct. 1988.

GARDNER, H. *The Mind's New Science.* New York: Basic Books, 1985.

INMON, W. H. *Information Systems Architecture.* Englewood Cliffs, N.J.: Prentice-Hall, Inc., 1986.

MARTIN, J. *Strategic Data-Planning Methodologies.* Englewood Cliffs, N.J.: Prentice-Hall, Inc., 1982.

MARTIN, J. *System Design from Provably Correct Constructs.* Englewood Cliffs, N.J.: Prentice Hall, Inc., 1986.

McCLURE, C. *CASE Is Software Automation.* Englewood Cliffs, N.J.: Prentice-Hall, Inc., 1989.

MILLER, G. A. "The Magical Number of Seven, Plus or Minus Two: Some limits to our capacity for processing information." *Psychological Review,* **63**, 1956, pp. 81-97.

NEWTON, J. J. "Guide on Data Entity Naming Conventions." *NBS Special Publication 500-149.* Gaithersburg, Md.: National Bureau of Standards, Oct. 1987.

PARNAS, D. L. "On the Criteria to Be Used in Decomposing Systems into Modules." *Commun. Assoc. Computer Machinery,* **15**, Dec. 1972, pp. 1053–58.

WEINBURG, G. M. *Psychology of Computer Programming.* New York: Van Nostrand Reinhold, 1971.

WEINER, N. *The Human Use of Human Beings.* Cambridge, Mass.: M.I.T. Press, 1952.

YOURDON, E. *Modern Structured Analysis.* Englewood Cliffs, N.J.: Yourdon Press, 1989.

ZACHMAN, J. A. "A Framework for Information Systems Architecture." *IBM Sys. J.,* **26**, No. 3, 1987. p. 22.

Index